T0384936

Using Generative AI Effectively in Higher Education

Using Generative AI Effectively in Higher Education explores how higher education providers can realise their role and responsibility in harnessing the power of generative artificial intelligence (GenAI) ethically and sustainably.

This rich collection of established and evaluated practices from across global higher education offers a practical guide to leading an agile institutional response to emerging technologies, building critical digital literacy across an entire institution, and embedding the ethical and sustainable use of GenAI in teaching, learning, and assessment. Including reflections from stakeholders testifying to the value of the approaches outlined, the book examines how higher education can equip staff and students with the critical-digital literacy necessary to use GenAI in work, study, and social life responsibly and with integrity. It provides an evidence-based resource for any kind of higher education (HE) provider (modern, college-based, and research-focused) looking for inspiration and approaches which can build GenAI capability and includes chapters on the development of cross-institutional strategy, policies and processes, pedagogic practices, and critical-digital literacy.

This resource will be invaluable to educational leaders, educational developers, learning developers, learning technologists, course administrators, quality assurance staff, and HE teachers wishing to embrace and adapt to a GenAI-enabled world.

Sue Beckingham is a National Teaching Fellow and Associate Professor at Sheffield Hallam University, UK.

Jenny Lawrence is Professor of Higher Education and Director of the Oxford Brookes Centre for Academic Enhancement and Development, UK. She is also Senior Fellow of SEDA, Principal and National Teaching Fellow.

Stephen Powell is a freelance Higher Education consultant based in New Zealand and Principal Fellow of AdvanceHE.

Peter Hartley is a freelance Higher Education consultant, National Teaching Fellow, and Visiting Professor at Edge Hill University, UK.

The Staff and Educational Development Association Focus Series

Series Editor: Stephen Powell

The SEDA Focus series is for everyone interested in teaching, learning and assessment in higher education. Books in the Series are scholarly and practical, written by educational developers and researchers on up-to-the minute topics, bringing together experience and practice in a theoretical context. The Series is for educational, academic, staff and faculty developers, subject academics developing their professional teaching interests, institutional managers and everyone working to improve the quality of student learning. SEDA (The Staff and Educational Development Association) is the long-established professional association for staff and educational developers in the UK, promoting innovation and good practice in higher education.

Titles in the series:

Active Learning in Higher Education
Theoretical Considerations and Perspectives
Edited by Wendy Garnham and Isobel Gowers

Perspectives on Teaching and Learning Leadership in Higher Education
Case Studies from UK and Australia
Edited by Josephine Lang, Namrata Rao and Anesa Hosein

Supporting the Student Journey into Higher Education
How Pre-Arrival Platforms Can Enhance Widening Participation
Edited by Wendy Garnham and Nina Walker

Using Generative AI Effectively in Higher Education
Sustainable and Ethical Practices for Learning, Teaching and Assessment
Edited by Sue Beckingham, Jenny Lawrence, Stephen Powell and Peter Hartley

For more information about this series, please visit: www.routledge.com/SEDA-Focus/book-series/SEDAF

Using Generative AI Effectively in Higher Education

Sustainable and Ethical Practices for Learning, Teaching and Assessment

Edited by
Sue Beckingham, Jenny Lawrence,
Stephen Powell and Peter Hartley

Routledge
Taylor & Francis Group

LONDON AND NEW YORK

First published 2024
by Routledge
4 Park Square, Milton Park, Abingdon, Oxon OX14 4RN

and by Routledge
605 Third Avenue, New York, NY 10158

Routledge is an imprint of the Taylor & Francis Group, an informa business

British Library Cataloguing-in-Publication Data
A catalogue record for this book is available from the British Library

ISBN: 978-1-032-77398-8 (hbk)
ISBN: 978-1-032-77403-9 (pbk)
ISBN: 978-1-003-48291-8 (ebk)

DOI: 10.4324/9781003482918

Typeset in Times New Roman
by Apex CoVantage, LLC

Contents

Contributors

Kathleen Armour
Kathleen is Vice Provost Education and Student Experience University College London, UK.

Sue Beckingham
Sue Beckingham is an Associate Professor, National Teaching Fellow, and Teaching and Learning Lead for the Department of Computing at Sheffield Hallam University, UK. She is also a Senior Fellow of the Higher Education Academy, a certified management and business educator, and a visiting fellow at Edge Hill University.

Tina Beynen
Dr Tina Beynen is a Lecturer in applied linguistics, writing coach, and certified language instructor specialising in English for academic purpose at Carleton University, Canada. Her research interests include the transition to university, higher education assessment, and student assessment literacies.

Pierce Burr
Pierce Burr is a neurosurgery Trainee in Leeds, UK and medical education enthusiast, holding degrees in medicine from St. Andrews University and Manchester University. Burr is committed to discovering enhanced learning experiences for medical professionals to improve patient outcomes.

Ceridwen Coulby
Ceridwen Coulby is Director of the Centre for Innovation in Education at the University of Liverpool, UK. She has worked in senior roles in both student experience and widening participation that have informed her student-centred approach to curriculum development and enhancement. Ceri has also spearheaded Liverpool's institutional response to generative AI technology in terms of policy and practice.

Mary Davis
Professor Mary Davis is Academic Integrity Lead and Professor (Student Experience) at Oxford Brookes University. A Principal Fellow HEA, she

focuses her research on inclusive educational approaches to academic integrity. She co-leads the International Day of Action for Academic Integrity.

Jayne Evans

Jayne Evans is an Academic Skills Manager, based in the UK, with a strong background in developing and delivering innovative student-led activities and a particular interest in working in partnership with students to ensure that all are able to thrive in higher education. She is keen to uphold the principles of meaningful co-creation, co-design, and co-production in her work with students.

Hazel Farrell

Coming from a background in analytical musicology, Hazel is actively involved in technology-enhanced learning, with research focused on student engagement in creative disciplines. Farrell's recent explorations involve the use of GenAI to enhance learning experiences.

Rachel Fitzgerald

Rachel Fitzgerald (PhD, SFHEA) is an Associate Professor and serves as an Associate Dean (Academic) at the University of Queensland, Australia. Her extensive knowledge in online education has earned her international acclaim for advancing digital learning, researching educational innovation, and improving the student learning experience.

Nigel Francis

Nigel Francis (SFHEA) is a Senior Lecturer focusing on enhancing immunology education. He is a National Teaching Fellow, and a winner of the Royal Society of Biology HE Educator of the Year award.

James L. Findon

James is a Senior Lecturer in psychology at King's College London, UK where he leads the Brain and Body Lab and the Education Research Group. His research focuses on co-occurring conditions in neurodevelopmental disorders, student mental health, and active learning techniques.

Rachel Forsyth

Rachel Forsyth, PFHEA, is an Educational Developer at Lund University in Sweden. Her recent book, *Confident Assessment in Higher Education* (Sage, 2022), is a practical guide for anyone working in higher education to understand and improve assessment. She is editor-in-chief of the Student Engagement in Higher Education Journal.

Peter Gossman

Peter is a Principal Lecturer in education and inclusion at the University of Worcester, UK.

Kimberley Hall

Kimberley Hall is an Associate Professor in English and digital media studies at Wofford College, US. Her research areas include social media discourse and culture and media and information literacy.

Kirsty Hemsworth

Dr Kirsty Hemsworth is an Academic Skills Manager with a passion for digitally enhanced teaching and working with students to co-design innovative academic skills initiatives at Sheffield Hallam University, UK. She holds a doctorate in translation studies from the University of Sheffield and is currently interested in deploying user experience methodologies to investigate how students navigate the intersections of academic and AI literacies.

Peter Hartley

Peter is Visiting Professor at Edge Hill University, UK, a National Teaching Fellow, and an independent educational consultant, with long-standing interests in human communication, group and organisational behaviour, and the application of new technologies in both educational and commercial organisations.

Noelle Hatley

Noelle Hatley has a diverse background encompassing design, account management, and buying. In 2012, she moved into education, culminating in a research-based master's degree exploring sustainability in fashion. She has successfully disseminated her findings through publications and broadcasts on both radio and television platforms. Noelle is dedicated to leveraging her extensive expertise and research insights to drive positive change and innovation in the fashion industry.

Claire Heard

Claire is a Lecturer in the Department of Psychology at King's College London, UK, Claire's research centres on exploring our judgement and decision-making, particularly risk perception and influences of choice architecture. She also investigates teaching and assessment, including artificial intelligence and assessment.

Julie Hodson

Julie Hodson is a Programme Leader, for fashion business and management, fashion marketing, fashion buying, and merchandising at Manchester Metropolitan University, UK.

Erhan Isik

Erhan is a quantity surveying and commercial management master's student, Oxford Brookes University, UK

Ajay Kumar

Ajay Kumar is currently a GP within the Caribbean Netherlands and a diploma student in clinical neurology at University College London, UK. He did his medical school from University College of Medical Sciences, Delhi, in India.

Jenny Lawrence

Jenny Lawrence is Principal Fellow of the Higher Education Academy, Senior Fellow of the Staff and Educational Development Association. Her research interests include educational leadership. She is a principal fellow, HEA, National Teaching Fellows, and a senior fellow of SEDA.

Evelyn Lai

Evelyn Lai is an education-focused Lecturer in banking and finance at the University of New South Wales, Australia. Her research interests focus on assessment and feedback design to encourage sustainable learning, edTech, and data-driven student learning experiences.

Rob Lindsay

Rob Lindsay is an Educational Developer in the University of Liverpool's Centre for Innovation in Education in the UK. He specialises in an inclusive approach to integrating technology within curriculum development to enhance the learning experience.

Jon Mason

Dr Jon Mason is an Associate Professor in Education at Charles Darwin University, Australia, where he lectures in digital technologies and teaching in higher education. His research interests span the frontiers of digital technology innovation, sense-making, questioning, standards development, and the getting of wisdom.

Ivy Chia Sook May

Dr Ivy Chia is an Associate Professor in education at Singapore University of Social Sciences. She actively engages in cross-disciplinary research, exploring a diverse array of subjects, including social media, blockchain technology, gamification strategies, and entrepreneurship initiatives.

Jennie Mills

Dr Jennie Mills is Associate Professor at the Academic Development Centre at the University of Warwick, UK. Her research explores the arts-based and post-qualitative pedagogies and practices within academic development and higher education research.

Lucy Myers

Lucy Myers is a Speech and Language Therapist who specialises in working with school-aged children with language impairment. Her research covers language and literacy.

Samantha Newell

Dr Samantha Newell is a Lecturer in psychology at the University of Adelaide, Australia. Her publications advance online learning through rapport, enhancing asynchronous engagement, promoting student voice, and facilitating student co-creation of learning spaces. She has published work that explores AI's impact on academic integrity.

Aaron O'Rourke

Aaron is a final-year music student, South East Technological University (SETU), Ireland.

Pauline Penny

Pauline Penny boasts a thriving career in buying, marketing, and product development within the fashion industry, culminating in senior management and leadership roles. Transitioning into the field of education six years ago, she holds a master's in higher education.

Jayne Pearson

Jayne is a Senior Lecturer in education in Kings Academy, Kings College, UK. Her main research interests are in assessment and feedback, particularly in the area of authentic and inclusive assessment design.

Stephen Powell

Stephen has worked in higher education for over 25 years, with a wide range of roles culminating in the head of the University Teaching Academy at Manchester Metropolitan University. He has a particular interest in using systems thinking to inquire into the workings of universities and applying this to teaching, learning, and assessment.

James Ciyu Qin

James Qin is a higher degree by research students studying systems engineering at the University of New South Wales, Australia.

Stian Reimers

Stian Reimers is a cognitive psychologist specialising in research on human decision-making. He also conducts research and develops technology around pedagogy and the student learning experience.

Charanjit Sangha

Charanjit is a BSc speech and language therapy student, City, University of London, UK.

Samuel Saunders

Samuel Saunders is an Educational Developer in the Centre for Innovation in Education at the University of Liverpool, UK. His research interests include authentic pedagogy, assessment and feedback, and decolonising the curriculum. Samuel also convenes the Generative Artificial Intelligence Network (GAIN).

David Smith

David Smith is a Professor of bioscience education. He is a National Teaching Fellow and a Principal Fellow of the Higher Education Academy. His innovative practice has been awarded the Royal Society of Biology HE Educator of the Year award.

Rebecca Upsher

In the Psychology Department at King's College London, UK, Rebecca's research centres on university student well-being within the curriculum, leading a global academic group on this. She also researches and informs university guidance on artificial intelligence and assessment.

Alex Walker

Alex is a recent graduate with a BSc (Hons) degree in geography. He is passionate about sustainable investment and has conducted research in collaboration with fund managers. Currently pursuing an MSc in finance and investment, Alex possesses global educational experience, including a role at a prominent Western Australian Boarding School, where he supported teaching and student growth.

Sumeyra Yalcintas

Dr Sumeyra Yalcintas is a Teaching Fellow at King's College London, UK, specialising in developmental psychology. Her research focuses on family dynamics, well-being, and close relationships. She also researches the role of artificial intelligence in learning and assessment.

Tim Young

Professor Tim Young leads clinical neurology degree courses at (University College London), UK. Qualifying as a medical doctor with triple distinction in 1997, he is an honorary consultant neurologist with a PhD in neuroscience and fellowships in clinical work (FRCP) and education (PFHEA).

Preface

Generative AI (GenAI) has made extraordinary advances over the last year, and there is every sign that it will continue to evolve at a rapid pace.

Our shared aim is to support the effective use of GenAI in teaching, learning, and assessment in ways which are appropriate to the context, including national regulations and requirements and institutionally specific policies.

This use of GenAI should be ethical, sustainable, and secure.

To meet these requirements, and recognising the ever-increasing pace of change, we need to be prepared to develop our practice in an uncertain environment.

As a result, we recommend that staff who wish to use GenAI (or are already using it) always check that they are following all the available institutional guidance on which tools to use and how.

1 Using generative AI effectively in higher education

Peter Hartley, Sue Beckingham, Jenny Lawrence, and Stephen Powell

Introduction

In less than a year, generative artificial intelligence (GenAI) developed from a specialist application of AI techniques to the ubiquitous technology which now dominates public debate about the impact of computers. *Collins Dictionary* described 'AI' as the 'word of the year' in 2023, the year when, on the one hand, we saw major computer companies like Microsoft and Google promising to embed AI in *all* their products (e.g. Endicott, 2023) while, on the other hand, we saw growing concerns about its long-term applications and implications, as in 'the world's first comprehensive EU legislation to regulate artificial intelligence' (O'Carroll, 2023).

GenAI is a technology that processes data to create entirely new text, audio, and images based on previous patterns of use, unlike retrieval AI used by search engines where existing relevant information is presented. The development of GenAI is seen as a major step towards artificial general intelligence (AGI) – where software can operate independently or autonomously, and where its capabilities match or exceed those of the best human operators. Although speedy, convenient tools that might liberate us from drudgery or enhance our creative capabilities, these applications are problematic. We can suggest a number of issues which all applications of GenAI should be aware of and should try to mitigate, namely that

- they further entrench colonial thinking by trawling dominating discourses to generate artefacts,
- they are exclusive as more sophisticated functions often sit behind paywalls,
- they are insecure as data pushed through some applications are used to inform future outputs,
- they are unreliable and produce 'hallucinations' based on patterns of language use not actual intelligence, and
- they are arguably a danger to society because they are 'morally naive' (Crook, 2022) and to the planet because the underpinning kit is so resource intensive (see Kumar and Davenport, 2023, for proposals to improve this situation).

DOI: 10.4324/9781003482918-1

However, we cannot ignore the 'power' of GenAI and its capacity to deliver outcomes which would be difficult if not impossible to achieve through other means. For example, Marr (2024) highlights the contribution that GenAI is making to efforts to resolve the climate crisis while also recognising its serious current impact on our natural resources.

One very clear trend is the increasing use of GenAI in both public and private organisations. For example, management consultants McKinsey described 2023 as "Generative AI's breakout year" in their report on the "explosive growth of . . . genAI tools" (McKinsey and Company, 2023). As a result, understanding and skills in the use of GenAI are fast emerging as an essential graduate skill, as anticipated by the World Economic Forum for some time (WEF, 2018).

In Higher Education (HE), we hold a responsibility to ensure AI is used for the common good (Fengchung and Holmes, 2023). We must furnish staff and students with the critical, digital literacies (Raley and Rhee, 2023), necessary to use GenAI ethically (Institute for Ethical AI in Education 2023) and with integrity (Foltynek et al., 2023) while being mindful of digital poverty (Illingsworth, 2023) and the moral and legal technicalities of data security (Department of Education, 2023). This will benefit students and the wider society, which they will shape as they reach their graduate destinations.

The growing number of predictions for the future of GenAI/AGI covers a very wide range – from the elimination of humanity and collapse of society to liberation from drudgery and enhanced creativity. Of course, HE institutions (HEIs) cannot escape this transformation, regardless of the outcome. All HEIs must now decide how to incorporate this new software into our educational portfolio and administrative processes and create the 'future-facing curricula' this fast-moving, fourth-industrial age requires (Huxley-Binns et al., 2023).

Our aims and objectives

The aim of this text is to support HEIs and learning communities to harness GenAI ethically and sustainably by providing practical, evidence-based guidance on the best ways to embed GenAI in teaching, learning, and assessment.

This collection of original chapters from universities across Europe and Australasia focuses on GenAI's educational significance and impact for HE. Each chapter ends with a short critical evaluation from a relevant and independent educator or student.

In 2023, we saw guidance emerging from HEIs and national educational agencies. For example, the United Nations Education, Scientific and Cultural Organisation (Fenchun and Homes, 2023), and, in the UK, the Russell Group of Universities issued its set of principles (Russell Group, 2023) on the use of AI (involving one of our contributors).

However, this guidance typically offers *general* principles without examples of specific educational practices. This book focuses on specific initiatives and practical examples that safely and ethically embrace the new technology.

GenAI is developing very fast. Our contributors all recognised the need for future-proofing – they focus on issues and possible solutions rather than detailed technical features. All our main topics have long shelf lives, including ethical use of technology, digital literacy, academic integrity, and authentic approaches to teaching and assessment. All these topics will create significant challenges for *all* HEIs for many years to come. We recommend that when using GenAI in teaching, learning, and assessment, teachers follow institutional guidance on which tools to use and how. This will ensure that the effective use of GenAI in a given nationally defined legal-regulatory and institutionally specific policy context is ethical, sustainable, and secure.

Contents

Part A: Institutional strategies for building generative AI capability

This part explores how HEIs have developed general strategies and frameworks to address GenAI's challenges and opportunities.

Chapter 2, by Samuel Saunders, Ceridwen Coulby, and Rob Lindsay, explores the challenges faced by the Centre for Innovation in Education (CIE), working to integrate GenAI at the University of Liverpool (UK). They highlight GenAI's role as a central hub for discussing, enhancing practices, and formulating policies. They emphasise the importance of fostering staff and student literacy as a guiding philosophy for effectively integrating GenAI into academic practices.

In Chapter 3, Mary Davis, from Oxford Brookes University (UK), starts from the growing recognition of the need for inclusive teaching and support in HE to address academic integrity challenges. As GenAI becomes more prevalent, universities must provide positive guidance to students on its appropriate use and address digital inequity concerns. This chapter outlines a tried-and-tested approach to this, including the implementation of transparent student declarations and institutional resources.

Part B: Developing GenAI literacy

This part explores how we can ensure that staff and students develop appropriate levels of 'GenAI literacy'. Each chapter explores different perspectives and different contexts, from changing staff attitudes and concerns regarding GenAI, through to particular students' uses and preconceptions of GenAI.

In Chapter 4, James Bedford, Mira Kim, and James Ciyu Qin, from the University of New South Wales (Australia), discuss GenAI's potential to support autonomous student learning. They highlight the impact of tools like ChatGPT-3.5/-4 on academic writing, focusing on English as Additional Language (EAL) students. They conclude that, when used responsibly, GenAI can enhance EAL student learning by providing effective support, fostering autonomy, and boosting confidence.

In Chapter 5, Samantha Newell and colleagues from universities in Australia, Canada, and the UK have collaborated to understand how equitable GenAI integration can address educational disparities and benefit HE. They critically examine the attitudes and practices of educators in integrating AI into their teaching, drawing on a wide range of real-world examples from a Facebook group for educators. They provide a taxonomy of GenAI use and examine potential future trends.

In Chapter 6, Kirsty Hemsworth, Jayne Evans, and Alex Walker, from Sheffield Hallam University (UK), discuss the intersection between GenAI tools and academic writing beyond issues of plagiarism, highlighting its potential to generate plausible written content. They explore how undergraduate students intuitively engage with ChatGPT and translate academic language into instructive prompts. They recommend strategies to support undergraduates using GenAI tools for academic writing.

Part C: Curriculum design for a GenAI-enabled world

This part offers case studies from four different disciplines that have engaged critically and ethically with GenAI. The authors describe their practice, reflect on their findings, and comment on likely future steps.

In Chapter 7, Hazel Farrell, from the South East Technological University (Ireland), focuses on creative approaches to student engagement in their music degree, utilising ChatGPT-3.5 and -4. The study evaluates how GenAI can support ideation, structuring, creation, evaluation, and feedback, with transferability and accessibility as core themes, and considers the integration of GenAI into authentic assessment models. The research promotes an inclusive platform for responsible-use discussions and investigates limitations and benefits.

In Chapter 8, Tim Young, Pierce Burr, and Ajay Kumar, University College London (UK), suggest that the potential of GenAI text-to-image generation remains underexplored. Medical education relies heavily on medical images, but challenges arise with rare conditions and issues of consent and confidentiality. Recent advances in text-to-image GenAI tools present an alternative approach – creating high-quality images from simple text prompts while ensuring patient confidentiality. They explore ethical considerations and provide examples of applications in medical education.

In Chapter 9, Stian Reimers and Lucy Myers, University of London (UK), use GenAI in group roleplay activities for their health sciences students. They developed a GPT-based roleplay app, allowing students to interact with an AI agent playing the role of a patient in a complex case, as part of a facilitated interprofessional learning day. The GenAI roleplay scenario provided challenges and discussion points, prompting students to handle support needs and professional agencies collaboratively.

In Chapter 10, Noelle Hatley and Pauline Penny from Manchester Metropolitan University (UK) integrated GenAI into their curriculum to enhance authenticity verification and authentic assessment practices. Their implementation in a first-year undergraduate unit spanned three programmes and engaged over 300 students. The assessment format included the PESTEL framework (a recognised analytical tool for examining environmental factors) and summarised learning outcomes, prompting students to analyse materials from different perspectives. Seminars and workshops involved ChatGPT to answer research questions.

Part D: Assessment in a GenAI-enabled world

This part focuses on assessment to enable students to confidently use GenAI effectively, ethically, and critically in context. It also considers the social value of meaningful authentic assessment.

In Chapter 11, Stephen Powell from Manchester Metropolitan University (UK) and Rachel Forsyth from Lund University (Sweden) review the fundamentals of assessment and feedback to provide the foundation to discuss the implications of GenAI for assessment design and management. They revise concepts of fairness, validity, and security regarding the affordances of GenAI tools and explore potential opportunities for GenAI across the assessment cycle, providing evidence-based guidance.

In Chapter 12, Rebecca Upsher and colleagues from King's College London (UK) critically examine the challenges, ethics, and opportunities of meaningfully incorporating GenAI into the context of authentic assessment. They use recent concepts of authenticity in HE assessment to explore affordances and challenges in the use of GenAI, beyond simply preparing students for the world of work. They provide a practical guide on how GenAI can shape student and staff experiences, rejuvenate assessment design, and stimulate broader discussions on the purpose of assessment in an ever-digitising world.

In Chapter 13, David Smith, Sheffield Hallam University (UK), and Nigel Francis, Cardiff University (UK), describe assessment designs where students are led through the creation process, starting with the identification of relevant content. Students log search strategies and keywords and evaluate the validity of the content. GenAI is then built into the assessment design by assessing the process, focusing on the justification of the resources used, and critiquing of the content material, be that books, articles, or AI-generated text.

Conclusion:
Sustainable and ethical AI for the common good

Finally, in Chapter 14, we suggest likely future developments in GenAI technology and reflect on how these may impact on the book's major theme – how we can adopt ethical, sustainable, and effective applications of GenAI with students across HE.

References

Crook. N (2022) *Rise of the Moral Machine: Exploring Virtue Through a Robot's Eyes*. UK. Amazon.

Department of Education (2023) *Policy Paper: Generative AI in Education*. UK: Department of Education. Available at: www.gov.uk/government/publications/generative-artificial-intelligence-in-education/generative-artificial-intelligence-ai-in-education (Accessed 30 January 2024).

Endicott, S. (2023) AI tools will be built into all Microsoft products, says CEO Satya Nadella. *Windows Central*. Available at: www.windowscentral.com/microsoft/ai-tools-will-be-built-into-all-microsoft-products-says-ceo-satya-nadella (Accessed 23 January 2024).

Fengchun, M. and Holmes, W. (2023) *Guidance for Generative AI in Education and Research*. United Nations Educational, Scientific and Cultural Organisation. Available at: https://unesdoc.unesco.org/ark:/48223/pf0000386693.locale=en (Accessed 1 February 2024).

Foltynek, T., Bjelobaba, S., Glendinning, I., Khan, Z.R., Santos, R., Pavletic, P. and Kravjar, J. (2023) ENAI Recommendations on the ethical use of artificial intelligence in education. *International Journal for Educational Integrity*, 19(12). Available at: https://doi.org/10.1007/s40979-023-00133-4.

Huxley-Binns, R. Lawrence, J. and Scott, G. (2023) Competence-based HE: Future proofing curricula. In Sengupta, E. (Ed.), *Integrative Curricula – A Multi-Dimensional Approach to Pedagogy*. UK: Emerald Group Publishing.

Illingsworth, S. (2023) If AI is to become a key tool in education, access has to be equal. *The Conversation*. Available at: https://theconversation.com/if-ai-is-to-become-a-key-tool-in-education-access-has-to-be-equal-204156#comment_2913535 (Accessed 30 November 2023).

Institute for AI in Education (2023) *The Ethical Framework for AI in Education*. Available at: The-Institute-for-Ethical-AI-in-Education-The-Ethical-Framework-for-AI-in-Education.pdf (buckingham.ac.uk) (Accessed 23 January 2024).

Kumar, A. and Davenport, T. (2023) How to make generative AI greener. *Harvard Business Review*. Available at: https://hbr.org/2023/07/how-to-make-generative-ai-greener#:~:text=Companies%20can%20take%20eight%20steps%20to%20make%20these,resources%3B%20include%20AI%20activity%20in%20your%20carbon%20monitoring (Accessed 28 January 2024).

Marr, B. (2024) Will generative AI help us solve the climate crisis (or will it make it worse)? *Forbes*. Available at: www.forbes.com/sites/bernardmarr/2024/01/25/will-generative-ai-help-us-solve-the-climate-crisis-or-will-it-make-it-worse/ (Accessed 28 January 2024).

McKinsey & Company (2023) *The State of AI in 2023: Generative AI's Breakout Year*. McKinsey & Company. Available at: www.mckinsey.com/capabilities/quantumblack/our-insights/the-state-of-ai-in-2023-generative-AIs-breakout-year (Accessed 28 January 2024).

O'Carroll, L. (2023) EU agrees 'historic' deal with world's first laws to regulate AI. *The Guardian*. Available at: www.theguardian.com/world/2023/dec/08/eu-agrees-historic-deal-with-worlds-first-laws-to-regulate-ai (Accessed 23 January 2024).

Raley, R and Rhee, J (2023) Critical AI: A Field in Formation. *American Literature*, 95(2), 185–204.

Russell Group (2023) New principles on use of AI in education. *Russell Group*. Available at: https://russellgroup.ac.uk/news/new-principles-on-use-of-ai-in-education/ (Accessed 23 January 2024).

World Economic Forum (2018) *The Future of Jobs Report 2018*. WEF. Available at: www.weforum.org/reports/the-future-of-jobs-report-2018.

Part A

Institutional strategies for building generative AI capability

2 Pedagogy and policy in a brave new world

A case study on the development of generative AI literacy at the University of Liverpool

Samuel Saunders, Ceridwen Coulby, and Rob Lindsay

Introduction

The Centre for Innovation in Education (CIE) at the University of Liverpool is a centralised service that enhances curriculum development through support with programme design, as well as via innovation in learning, teaching, and assessment (CIE, n.d.-a). CIE is also responsible for the development and implementation of digital education initiatives.

When GenAI emerged into the mainstream in late 2022 (OpenAI, 2022), we quickly realised both its potential and its possible danger to academic integrity. While it was an exciting (if daunting) prospect, most academic and professional colleagues perceived GenAI as a threat. How effective would traditional assessments be? How would staff know if students had produced their own work? And who had the answers to these questions?

At that time, *nobody* had the answers, and even at the time of writing (January 2024), universities are still wrestling with these issues – as are influential UK voices such as the Quality Assurance Agency (QAA) and the Department for Education (DfE). Consequently, managing GenAI was, and remains, a matter of exploring the technology, collaborating with colleagues, and staging discussions to identify both potential answers to some of these questions and *further* questions to ask, and what epistemic shifts we need in this uncertain environment.

The Satir Model

The Satir Change Model (Satir et al., 1991) is a psychological framework, describing the process individuals and systems undergo in response to (often unexpected or significant) change. Its five stages, summarised below, effectively capture our experience responding to GenAI.

DOI: 10.4324/9781003482918-3

Late status quo

There is balance, events proceed as normal, and those within the system are comfortable.

Resistance

An unexpected element enters, typically causing confusion, uncertainty, and perhaps refusal to accept. Those within the system may feel threatened or anxious as they try to understand and manage change, although responses are not always consistent; some may welcome the disruption as an opportunity for innovation and growth. These advocates play a fundamental role in adaptation, although the inconsistent nature of resistance also complicates the landscape.

Chaos

As the element becomes embedded, some processes, practices, and systems begin to yield worse (or no) results, leading to experimentation. One or more 'transformative ideas' occur, leading to a new understanding that enables those within the system to envisage futures. This stage therefore includes 'light-bulb' moments, marking transitions from confusion to clarity for some, while others still struggle.

Integration and practice

The new idea or change is integrated into existing systems (though, again, it is not always accepted by everyone *simultaneously*). Practices are adapted or adjusted, but the integration is not a singular shift.

New status quo

A new equilibrium arises from the acceptance of the reality and/or permanence of the unexpected element. This does not necessarily indicate a state of *harmony*; rather, it refers to a dynamic, evolving state of acceptance and adaptation within the system that leaves it open to future changes/disruptions.

The Satir model highlights how chaos and discomfort are natural parts of change. By recognising this, we are more likely to find transformative growth.

A world before ChatGPT: Late status quo

In education, the 'late status quo' is where existing practices, technologies, and systems are well-established and accepted (or at least tolerated) by stakeholders, including teachers, administrators, and students.

COVID-19 was the last 'unexpected element' affecting education (pre-GenAI) which educators had to contend with. This had dramatic effects on the constitution and implementation of educational technology, leading to wider acceptance of virtual, online, and hybrid forms of teaching, learning, and assessment (Sharaievska et al., 2022). By late 2022, this disruption had somewhat abated, and an uneasy status quo re-emerged. Most HEIs, including Liverpool, now use a blended approach to programme delivery (Sharma and Shree, 2023).

Resistance to unexpected element

That said, higher education has often been hesitant to adopt digital transformations and integrate new technologies into teaching (Marks and Al-Ali, 2022). GenAI's appearance was no exception – predictably, 'resistance' appeared across all faculties, comprising four observable threads:

- A desire to outlaw the technology (particularly from especially vulnerable areas, such as subjects with assessments/activities that GenAI can easily complete (e.g. coding, translation, or data analysis))
- Indifference to the technology (particularly from subjects assessing reflection, creation, or originality), either due to limited understanding of GenAI's capability or because it was considered less effective
- Desire to return to traditional assessments – particularly examinations – as the supposed sole means of maintaining academic integrity
- Awareness of issues surrounding the technology, but few practical ideas on how to resolve them, combined with a strong desire for a solution to appear from the expertise of another party

These voices were unified in one respect: GenAI was 'a problem' requiring 'a solution'. But in every other way, the 'resistance' to GenAI bred pedagogic conflict refracted by disciplinary context. As a result, there was no discernible consensus on what to do about the technology. This prompted those *required* to respond to the technology to implement activities designed to explore, analyse, and ultimately understand the technology and its implications for pedagogy. 'Resistance' thus became 'chaos'.

Chaos

'Chaos' may seem too strong a term to describe the activities, by both CIE and academic staff, to try and manage GenAI's advent. However, when considered theoretically (i.e. where a process is said to be 'chaotic' if it is subject to unobservable uncertainties that make its outcome impossible to predict (Ivancevic and Ivancevic, 2008)), it is *exactly* the correct term.

Once increasing numbers of staff began to (a) become aware of GenAI and (b) become convinced, it was here to stay, thoughts turned to predictions of its effects on pedagogy. But this was impossible; predictions were embedded in both specific disciplinary practices (rather than inter- or multi-disciplinary contexts) and, simultaneously, based on assumptions about how the technology would potentially fit into existing structures (rather than how it might develop new (or *adapt* existing) ones).

The single unifying thought that emerged was that we needed a dedicated, open, and safe space to discuss and critique the potential benefits, dangers, and ethical implications of the technology. This led to the establishment of the 'Assistive Technology Working Group' (ATWG), a subset of the Assessment and Feedback Working Group (AFWG) (which has significant influence over both policy and practice in assessment/feedback).

The ATWG has been very useful, largely because of its significant voice (via AFWG) and because it consists of representatives from across the institution, allowing both broad collaboration and quick dissemination. It brought together a wide range of stakeholders – from in-department Assessment and Academic Integrity Officers to Academic Quality staff. Students were also involved, both via the Guild of Students and (in particular) through a staff/student partnership project run by the Library.

Ethical implications around GenAI became one of the ATWG's key focuses. Discussions here tended to fall into three categories:

- Ethics of what goes *into* GenAI.

    There are substantial questions about how, and by whom, data has been fed into GenAI models, especially regarding OpenAI's ChatGPT (Catania, 2023).
- Ethics of what comes *out* of GenAI.

    Concerns around authorship and ownership of GenAI content are unresolved (Zohny et al., 2023), as are concerns around evident political, social, racial, and cultural biases (Alba, 2022).
- Ethics of access to GenAI.

    Gaps widen between those with infrastructure and financial ability to pay for applications/services and those who cannot (Seah, 2020).

Through collaboration with the Educational Development Unit at Liverpool's partner institution, Xi'an Jiaotong-Liverpool University (XJTLU), the group decided to emphasise the importance of user privacy, fair and equitable access, and transparency in GenAI applications. We sought to ensure that GenAI's benefits *reached* all students, as this would allow us to more consciously use GenAI to help students with diverse accessibility requirements to better access their course in the future.

At the time of writing, we are seeking an enterprise licence to enable equitable access to the most up-to-date version of ChatGPT. That said, as the landscape of GenAI evolves, our considerations remain flexible. We will adapt to the latest advancements and ethical challenges.

The most substantial part of the ATWG's remit was to create and disseminate a university 'position' on GenAI use. There was a lack of awareness around what was and was not (or 'should' and 'should not be') permissible when using GenAI – both for students and staff.

The group collectively produced two sets of University 'Position Papers' – in February and May 2023; each with staff and student-facing aspects, published on the CIE website. They were designed to not only (a) provide immediate clarity on the use of GenAI on interdisciplinary levels but also (b) provide the group more time to produce more comprehensive, research-informed policy for the intermediate-to-long term.

These papers reflect our journey through the Satir model. In the first, GenAI use was prohibited unless permitted by the module tutor. On reflection, this position was grounded in 'resistance' and quickly became untenable; on the one hand, we could not accurately verify whether a student had used GenAI in their assessment (in many ways, we still cannot – Turnitin's detector tool was not then operational and has not yet proven its effectiveness since coming online), while third-party detection software was not ethically or pedagogically viable (Rahimi and Abadi, 2023). On the other, our understanding of GenAI was developing almost every day, alongside advances in the technology itself, and it became evident that it was, in essence, here to stay.

The second paper therefore focused more strongly on appropriate *use* of GenAI, centred on educating staff and students about its benefits and limitations and guiding its appropriate citation (CIE., n.d.-b). It essentially 'endorsed' the use of GenAI (in the right contexts and via the right practices) which necessitated the development of more comprehensive policy around academic integrity and examination conduct (now approved and incorporated into Liverpool's Code of Practice on Assessment (CoPA).

With GenAI set to become ubiquitous within the academy and without (Saunders, 2023), thoughts turned to sustainable integration of the technology into pedagogy. CIE-led experimentation with, and discussion of, several tools yielded some initial ideas, such as generating authentic scenarios for assessments; manipulating lengthy text; providing prompts or ideas for structuring assessments; or providing a space to explore or discuss possibilities for how the technology might change the world in the future (Carvalho et al., 2022). A space was needed to share these ideas, and so CIE organised several 'Generative AI: Beyond the Fear' events – discussion groups where participants related their experiences with GenAI and discussed these ideas for its integration.

However, somewhat unexpectedly, this was also not sustainable. Numerous participants responded to CIE's suggestions/ideas with the point that disciplinary distinctions rendered them obsolete, unworkable, or too complex. In retrospect, a central service suggesting specific practices for using the technology in an interdisciplinary space was largely bound to come up against this issue (Zhu et al., 2023).

This prompted two shifts in approach: to implement more discipline-focused activities and to provide teaching academics with space to figure out *for themselves* how the technology would work best in their own pedagogic contexts.

As a result, our underlying philosophy began to revolve around *AI literacy*. It was simply not possible for CIE to provide training, knowledge, resources, or expertise to every disciplinary context, nor would it be sustainable in the long term. Rather, it was up to academics to understand the technology for themselves in their own context, before similarly developing students' discipline-specific AI literacy (more generic support for students was developed by the Library).

Students' GenAI literacy is also critically important to Liverpool; the Liverpool Curriculum Framework (LCF) includes both the Hallmarks of the curriculum and Graduate Attributes (CIE, n.d.-c). This includes 'Digital Fluency' as a characteristic that Liverpool instils in students. Without GenAI Literacy, students simply cannot become 'digitally fluent'.

This underpinning philosophy of 'literacy over practice' directly informed the wider Russell Group response to the advent of GenAI (Russell Group, 2023). It also helped to focus CIE's efforts and acted as the 'transformative idea' (Satir et al., 1991) that helped orient our efforts into a structured and workable strategy. As a result, 'Chaos' became 'Integration'.

Integration and practice

The focus on literacy allowed CIE to progress from the 'Beyond the Fear' workshops to provide more universally helpful support. New sessions provided a brief introduction to GenAI, its developments, and potential futures, followed by interactive spaces where participants could experiment with the technology in their own way, with CIE staff present to assist. Three hyflex workshops were designed and delivered over the summer months of 2023, repeated in 2024/25.

Elsewhere, it was fortunate that the conclusion to focus on literacy was reached before the end of the second semester of AY 2022–23. Towards the end of the term, CIE began to receive a substantial number of requests from academic departments for sessions at awaydays themed around GenAI and integration into the curriculum. We delivered around 30 talks and events across the university between May and July 2023, all centred on developing AI literacy.

This revised approach for workshops, away day sessions, and CPD has been far more successful than our first efforts, evidenced through both participant feedback and subsequent collaborative projects to embed AI into pedagogy. Crucially, though, it is also more *sustainable* and open to repeated delivery/attendance as GenAI inevitably changes. With new iterations, such as Microsoft's Copilot, the way that the technology is accessed and used will become less conscious; users will naturally use GenAI when they perform as basic a function as a web search or write a paragraph in a word processor. As the technology changes, then, so too will pedagogy, and providing access to dedicated and unstructured spaces for academics to experientially explore changes in the technology that might affect their practice is critically important in the intermediate-to-long term (Kolb, 2014).

Finally, we note that concerns will inevitably extend beyond the classroom. Students may, for example, be apprehensive about how GenAI will impact their job prospects, the dynamics of their chosen professions, and its broader societal implications. To this end, CIE has partnered with careers and employability to equip careers coaches with the knowledge, skills, and confidence to effectively leverage GenAI tools in the Career Studio.

Conclusion: The new status quo

In Satir et al.'s (1991) 'New Status Quo', what was once disruptive becomes accepted as the new normal. Those who resisted change became accustomed to it.

Neither we nor the sector have reached this stage regarding GenAI. Many have accepted the need to integrate the technology into their practice, but many staff are still fearful or resistant.

In a true 'new status quo', GenAI literacy will be a core skill that universities work to develop among students to ensure that they graduate with the skills they need to succeed in the rest of their personal and professional lives. In broader terms, 'new status quo' will also witness the higher education community's reconceptualisation of the concept of academic integrity to a 'post plagiarism' position (Eaton, 2021) that accounts for the inevitable blurring of human and machine-generated material.

However, perhaps the very idea of a 'new status quo' should be challenged? The COVID-19 pandemic created a situation where many traditional face-to-face educational practices became obsolete, instigating an unprecedented pace of development in online, hybrid, and digital pedagogies (Vargo et al., 2021). In 2024, we are experiencing another seismic shift in education with the growth of GenAI. Perhaps, then, there are no 'static' moments. Instead, we simply need to accept the wisdom of Heraclitus that the only constant in life, and in education, is change.

Stakeholder appraisal

Tom Rutherford, Advocacy Manager, Liverpool Guild of Students

In my role as Advocacy Manager within the Liverpool Guild of Students, I have witnessed first-hand the emergence of GenAI use among the student body at the University. This started from a position of novelty prior to the release of ChatGPT and the accompanying media coverage. Following this, it became clear that the university would need to respond with clear guidance for staff and students.

It is positive then that the CIE have played such an active role in the University's response as this has ensured a focus on benefits for enhancing the teaching and learning experience, as opposed to a purely punitive approach. In particular, I have found CIE's focus on developing GenAI literacy among staff and students to be particularly valuable, as this will allow people to develop their own skills and confidence using GenAI while accepting that not everyone is starting from an equal position. This, alongside a commitment to ensuring equitable access to the technology, shows that inclusivity has been at the centre of the university response, something that students were keen to see.

There remain significant challenges around ensuring students are clear about what constitutes acceptable practice as the technology becomes more embedded and this approach is implemented. As assessment practices start to develop, what is deemed acceptable GenAI use may become assessment specific, varying between different modules. This has the potential to create confusion for students especially where courses cover multiple discipline areas. Students will also continue to enter the university with differing experiences of what is considered acceptable GenAI use. CIE's focus, however, on developing GenAI literacy among staff and students should ensure the University is well placed to respond to these challenges as the technology continues to develop.

References

Alba, D. (2022) OpenAI chatbot spits out biased musings despite guardrails. *Bloomberg*, 8 December. Available at: www.bloomberg.com/news/newsletters/2022-12-08/chatgpt-open-ai-s-chatbot-is-spitting-out-biased-sexist-results (Accessed 12 January 2024).

Carvalho, L., Martinez-Maldonado, R., Tsai, Y., Markauskaite, L. and De Laat, M. (2022) How can we design for learning in an AI world? *Computers and Education: Artificial Intelligence*, 3(1). Available at: https://doi.org/10.1016/j.caeai.2022.100053 (Accessed 26 January 2024).

Catania, J. (2023) Slave labour in the data mines of ChatGPT. *3CL Foundation*, 19 June. Available at: www.3cl.org/slave-labour-in-the-data-mines-of-chatgpt/ (Accessed 12 January 2024).

Centre for Innovation in Education (n.d.-a) *About Us*. Available at: www.liverpool.ac.uk/centre-for-innovation-in-education/about-us/ (Accessed 12 January 2024).

Centre for Innovation in Education (n.d.-b) *Acceptable and Unacceptable Uses of Generative Artificial Intelligence in Assessment – Guidance for Staff and Students*. Available at: www.liverpool.ac.uk/media/livacuk/centre-for-innovation-in-education/digital-education/generative-ai-teach-learn-assess/acceptable-unacceptable-use-gai-guidance-staff-students.pdf (Accessed 15 January 2024).

Centre for Innovation in Education (n.d.-c) *Liverpool Curriculum Framework*. Available at: www.liverpool.ac.uk/centre-for-innovation-in-education/curriculum-resources/ (Accessed 12 January 2024).

Eaton, S. E. (2021) *Plagiarism in Higher Education: Tackling Tough Topics in Academic Integrity*. New York, NY: Bloomsbury Publishing.

Ivancevic, V. and Ivancevic, T. (2008) *Complex Linearity: Chaos, Phase Transitions, Topology Change and Path Integrals*. Springer Berlin, Heidelberg.

Kolb, D. (2014) *Experiential Learning: Experience as the Source of Learning and Development*, 2nd ed. New Jersey: Pearson.

Marks, A. and Al-Ali, M. (2022) Digital transformation in higher education: A framework for maturity assessment. In Alaali, M. (Ed.), *COVID-19 Challenges to University Information Technology Governance*. Switzerland: Springer Chem.

OpenAI (2022) Introducing ChatGPT. *Official OpenAI Blog*, 30 November. Available at: https://openai.com/blog/chatgpt (Accessed 12 January 2024).

Rahimi, F. and Abadi, A.T.B. (2023) ChatGPT and publication ethics. *Archives of Medical Research*, 54(3). Available at: https://doi.org/10.1016/j.arcmed.2023.03.004 (Accessed 26 January 2024).

Russell Group (2023) *Russell Group Principles on the Use of Generative AI Tools in Education*. Available at: https://russellgroup.ac.uk/media/6137/rg_ai_principles-final.pdf (Accessed 12 January 2024).

Satir, V., Banmen, J., Gerber, J. and Gomori, M. (1991) *The Satir Model: Family Therapy and Beyond*. Palo Alto, CA: Science and Behaviour Books.

Saunders, S. (2023) Rather than ban generative AI, universities must learn from the past. *University World News*, 24 February. Available at: https://tinyurl.com/3b43ahmr (Accessed 12 January 2024).

Seah, K.M. (2020) COVID-19: Exposing digital poverty in a pandemic. *International Journal of Surgery*, 79, pp. 127–128. Available at: https://doi.org/10.1016/j.ijsu.2020.05.057 (Accessed 26 January 2024).

Sharaievska, I., McAnirilin, O., Browning, M., Larson, L., Mullenbach, L., Rigolon, A., D'Antonio, A., Cloutier, S., Thomsen, J., Covelli Metcalf, E. and Reigner, N. (2022) 'Messy transitions': Students' perspectives on the impacts of the COVID-19 pandemic on higher education. *Higher Education*. Available at: https://doi.org/10.1007/s10734-022-00843-7 (Accessed 12 January 2024).

Sharma, L. and Shree, S. (2023) Exploring the online and blended modes of learning for post-COVID-19: A study of higher education institutions. *Education Sciences*, 13(2), p. 142. Available at: https://doi.org/10.3390/educsci13020142 (Accessed 26 January 2024).

Vargo, D., Zhu, L., Benwell, B. and Yan, Z. (2021) Digital technology use during COVID-19 pandemic: A rapid review. *Human Behavior and Emerging Technologies*, 3(1), pp. 13–24. Available at: https://doi.org/10.1002/hbe2.242 (Accessed 26 January 2024).

Zhu, G., Fan, X., Hou, C., Zhong, T., Seow, P., Shen-Hsing, A., Rajalingam, P., Yew, L.K. and Poh, T.L. (2023) Embrace opportunities and face challenges: Using ChatGPT in undergraduate students' collaborative disciplinary learning. *Computers and Society*. Available at: https://doi.org/10.48550/arXiv.2305.18616 (Accessed 26 January 2024).

Zohny, H., McMillan, J. and King, M. (2023) Ethics of generative AI. *Journal of Medical Ethics*, 49, pp. 79–80. Available at: http://dx.doi.org/10.1136/jme-2023-108909 (Accessed 26 January 2024).

3 Supporting inclusion in academic integrity in the age of GenAI

Mary Davis

Introduction

The need for more inclusive teaching and support to help students navigate academic integrity in higher education has begun to receive more attention in recent years (Davis, 2022; Eaton, 2022). It has been established that some student groups experience more difficulty in understanding and following academic integrity and therefore may be more susceptible to possible academic conduct breaches (Lynch et al., 2021). These student groups are likely to include neurodiverse students, students from widening participation backgrounds, international students, and certain ethnic groups, all of whom benefit from additional inclusive support (Davis, 2023).

Institutional policy responses that are led by warnings and threats can be extremely counter-productive especially to these student groups, as they perpetuate fear of sanctions, rather than desire for learning (Abasi and Graves, 2008). In addition, as pointed out by Leask (2006, p. 192):

> If the concept itself is not understood and/or students don't know what to do, or can't do what they have to do to avoid it, no deterrent will be effective.

With the advent of GenAI, unfortunately, some initial responses by universities have taken the form of Draconian threat:

> If you use AI, you will fail with 0% (UK university example).

This kind of threat ignores student needs for inclusion and support to follow good academic practice. On the other hand, positive ways to engage students with GenAI are starting to be promoted, for example, funding staff–student projects (King's College London, 2023). Thus, instead of increasing student anxiety and uncertainty about how to approach their assignments, in this

DOI: 10.4324/9781003482918-4

chapter, I argue for institutions to prioritise student inclusion with GenAI. I present three ways to focus on inclusion: first, by providing clear guidance for transparent use of GenAI; second, by incorporating Universal Design for Learning (UDL) principles (CAST, 2018) in an educational resource to help students navigate GenAI; and third, by examining ways to address digital inequity with GenAI.

Transparency

Transparency is one of the expected elements of academic integrity and research ethics. Students are expected to show attribution to any source of information that they use. Pecorari and Shaw (2012, p. 158) defined this as 'conventional intertextuality' in which a student writer signals the relationships between texts clearly through attribution in accordance with academic conventions, expected writer responsibility, and good practice. This is in contrast to 'deceptive intertextuality' where these relationships are not revealed by the writer through a lack of attribution. The importance of transparency to good practice is also highlighted by the International Center for Academic Integrity (ICAI) in defining the fundamental value of trust as:

(promoting) transparency in values, processes and outcomes.

(ICAI, 2019, p. 6)

This draws attention to transparency by not only students but also staff and institutions so that learning communities can be formed based on trust.

The European Network for Academic Integrity (ENAI) developed recommendations on the ethical use of GenAI linked to existing academic integrity values:

All persons, sources and tools that influence the ideas or generate the content should be properly acknowledged. Consequently, when an AI tool is used, it should be acknowledged.

(Foltynek et al., 2023)

It is essential for institutions to communicate clear, simple, and positive guidance on how to acknowledge the use of GenAI to avoid deceptive use; otherwise, as reported by Christou (2023, p. 1981) in the context of research:

fears are growing over the negligence or deliberate avoidance by researchers to refer to (AI) usage. Researchers . . . may not acknowledge the use of AI in their methodology . . . (due to) "fear" of being exposed to criticism.

Therefore, in line with the ENAI recommendation to:

> guide the users on how to correctly and transparently acknowledge the use of AI tools in an assignment.
>
> (Foltynek et al., 2023)

and in my role as academic integrity lead at my institution, I developed a simple declaration form, directly accessible at the point of assignment submission, requiring students to declare which AI tool they had used and how. The form was designed in this way to be straightforward and easy for all students to use and to remove fear or concerns about declaring AI tools. While there may be other means of facilitating transparency, the use of this declaration form also enabled the institution to monitor student use of GenAI. The subsequent declarations submitted by students by 496 students over a seven-month period (February–August 2023) about how they were actually using GenAI enabled me to then create a teaching resource detailed in the following section.

Navigation of academic integrity in GenAI

In order for all students to understand ethical approaches to GenAI in higher education, it is essential to provide guidance that is '*accessible, relevant and engaging*' (Thomas and May, 2010). UDL principles have become popular as a way to build in inclusion to make all teaching and learning materials accessible to all from the start, rather than adapting them later for some students, thus avoiding the social model of disability where the environment creates the disability (Brown and Leigh, 2020). The usefulness of applying UDL to learning about academic integrity has also begun to be recognised (Davis, 2022; Eaton, 2022). In my research, a student who self-reported as being neurodiverse and from a widening participation background stated regarding academic integrity:

> It is quite overwhelming when you have been out of education for a while, trying to take in the dos and don'ts.
>
> (Davis, 2022)

The need for greater inclusion and accessibility prompted me previously to apply UDL to academic integrity policies, procedures, and teaching to successfully support the institution in meeting its inclusivity goals (Davis, 2022, 2023). Consequently, I found it equally valuable to apply UDL to teaching all students about GenAI. I also realised that the most straightforward and accessible way of developing guidance for students on GenAI would be to embed it as a section of the already well-established in-house online academic integrity course.

Following the introduction of the declaration form detailed above, over a seven-month period, I analysed and categorised the student declarations of AI use into appropriate, at risk, and inappropriate. I used these categories to create a teaching resource as part of the module, guided by the four UDL principles of comprehension, with a traffic light system to help students navigate GenAI and stop, check, or go, respectively (see Table 3.1).

With their universal meaning in terms of colours and order of red, amber, and green meaning stop, check, and go, traffic lights are very commonly used to clarify concepts and check understanding, for example, McCormick and Harvey's (2018) Traffic Lights Toolkit in higher education. The traffic light system can thus help students to easily understand and differentiate between the categories through examples of appropriate and ethical AI use (such as using AI to define key terms or checking grammar), deceptive, and/or inappropriate use (e.g. generating the complete assignment and submitting the output as their own), and at risk use which may become inappropriate (such as using AI to create parts of an assignment). Table 3.2 displays the traffic light system (without the colours) and keywords highlighted in bold.

To ensure that students with colour vision deficiency are not disadvantaged, the different categories are also signalled by their consistent order, headings, and with symbols commonly used in learning settings of a tick ☑, question mark?, and cross ☒.

Having presented the categories in this accessible format, I then designed an exercise for students to apply their traffic light learning by identifying

Table 3.1 UDL application to traffic light resource

UDL Principle of Comprehension (CAST, 2018)	Application to traffic light resource
1. Activate or supply background knowledge	• Include introduction about AI and its prevalence in HE • Explain why guidance is needed
2. Highlight patterns, critical features, big ideas, and relationships	• Introduce concept of traffic lights as model to understand inappropriate, at risk, and appropriate use (stop, check, and go)
3. Guide information processing and visualisation	• Set out guidance in order and colour • Use layout and concept of traffic lights • Incorporate consistent symbols of tick, question mark, and cross for the three categories of appropriate use, at risk use, and inappropriate use
4. Maximise transfer and generalisation	• Check understanding through questions to reflect on examples that relate to different student practices

Table 3.2 Traffic light guidance for the use of GenAI

✓ Appropriate use	? At risk practices	✗ Inappropriate use
✓ **Ethical** use where the student is still the author of the assignment	? Relying on AI tools for a significant part of the assignment	✗ **Unethical** use where the student is no longer the author of the assignment
✓ **Transparent** use where the student makes clear where and how they have used AI in their assignment	? Not making all use of AI tools clear	✗ **Deceptive, hidden use** where the student uses AI but does not declare it with their assignment
✓ Helping the student **get started** with the assignment with planning or ideas	? Using AI tools to generate a part of the assignment	✗ Putting **the whole assignment task** into an artificial intelligence tool and using what is generated with little or no changes
✓ Helping the student **with small changes** in the development of their assignment such as correcting spelling	? Using AI for a lot of the development of an assignment	✗ Asking an AI tool to **generate a reference list** instead of the student doing research
✓ Helping the student with **proofreading**/ checking before submission of the assignment	? Using AI to re-write an assignment at the final stage	✗ Using AI tools to answer **exam questions**
✓ Using AI tools **with instruction or guidance from the tutor**	? Using AI in ways the tutor has not recommended	✗ Using AI when the assignment instructions state that **AI must not be used**

appropriate, at risk, or inappropriate practice in a set of authentic examples taken from the student declarations. The course was rolled out to all students at the beginning of the academic year 2023/24; promotions and reminders to prioritise taking it have helped to reach 3,300 completions in the first three months (our academic staff and student population is approximately 15,000). Feedback received from students suggests that traffic lights are welcome and an effective way to guide student understanding and navigation of GenAI, thus reducing anxiety over decisions related to GenAI. Staff feedback has demonstrated satisfaction with the availability of the course as a source of general institutional guidance that they can apply to their module information and assignment briefs. I have acknowledged the need for ongoing revisions as GenAI and student practices evolve, as well as the importance of adaptation, in order to respond to staff requests for additional detail for certain disciplines (particularly creative subjects) and for research students (e.g. about original contributions).

Digital inequity

Concerns about a number of factors causing digital inequity with GenAI are significant (JISC, 2023). Recent research has confirmed the need to take an equity lens to GenAI (Kaplan and Ravanera, 2022). Access can be the primary concern, as although promoted as open access tools for all, in fact the more advanced versions of AI tools are already behind a paywall which excludes students due to digital poverty (Illingsworth, 2023). Therefore, it is incumbent upon universities to consider providing access to GenAI tools to all students for appropriate use in the future (UNESCO, 2023).

However, digital inequity includes additional problems beyond access to AI tools. As argued by Zajko (2022), social inequalities can be amplified in AI as it is trained on algorithms based on potential human bias and discrimination. Marginalised populations including women or gender minorities, racialised, or low-income communities have been found to be poorly represented (Kaplan and Ravanera, 2022). Therefore, the output from GenAI may reinforce stereotypes and exclude those not actively involved in the development of technology (Sample Ward and Bruce, 2023). Yet, if all students are not given opportunities to use it in their learning, this disadvantages them both individually by preventing them from gaining key employability skills for their future careers (Foltynek et al., 2023) and collectively by stopping them shaping AI in society (Sample Ward and Bruce, 2023). Universities clearly need to use their position to decrease the digital divide by providing opportunities to use GenAI ethically to all students (Božić, 2023).

There are a number of initiatives to promote the positive, ethical use of GenAI in higher education, such as the organisation 'AI For Good' which advocates for AI in education to drive changes towards a more inclusive society to the benefit of all (Kalejs, 2023). As suggested by Illingsworth (2023), institutions can partner with community organisations to help students with access to technology. Furthermore, a large-scale project by Eaton et al. (2023) demonstrates a UDL framework for ethical and accessible teaching practices with GenAI.

Other recommended ways for institutions to promote digital equity in GenAI include ensuring programmes that provide adequate teaching and discussion of digital literacy skills (Illingsworth, 2023) and facilitating student use of institutional resources and services, which has been found to increase student sense of belonging (Davis, 2022). This is important because it is known that certain student groups may struggle with digital literacy and the same groups, especially neurodiverse or international students may not seek help from institutional services (Davis, 2022). Thus, institutions need to provide active support with digital skills and appropriate use of AI tools to empower the development of the entire student body.

Conclusion

An inclusive approach to academic integrity and GenAI has been discussed in this chapter through an institutional example with three elements. First, transparency in the use of GenAI through declaration forms was presented as an essential first step in supporting students to follow good practice. Second, a method to help students navigate GenAI was recommended through providing a traffic light teaching tool to distinguish between appropriate, at risk, and inappropriate practice, based on the UDL principles for comprehension. Third, the importance of institutions addressing digital inequity in GenAI was discussed. The three approaches have facilitated an inclusive and positive institutional response to the ongoing development of student practices with GenAI at Brookes that is building student GenAI literacy, as outlined in the student critical appraisal.

It is acknowledged that the recommendations here have been developed in the early stage of responses to the surge of use of GenAI in higher education and, consequently, are in the process of ongoing evaluation. The recommendations are grounded in the researcher's knowledge of inclusion in academic integrity, as well as the experience of an institution with a strong strategic focus on inclusivity and 10 months evolving our processes in response to student and staff use and feedback. Therefore, it is hoped that they prove useful to other institutions as they consider their approaches to the ethical use of GenAI by all students.

Critical appraisal

Erhan Isik, quantity surveying and commercial management master's student, Oxford Brookes University, UK

As a previous pre-master's and current master's student, GenAI has significantly streamlined various aspects of my life, in terms of understanding assignments and better communication through my emails. But, this integration of GenAI brings with it a complex mix of advantages and disadvantages that highlight the need for guidance and awareness for its appropriate and ethical use.

The introduction of the student declaration form is a practical step towards promoting transparency and accountability. In my opinion, distinguishing between group tasks and individual tasks not only improves collaboration within the group but also integrates a sense of self-control in the use of GenAI. In addition, filling out such a short form during assignment submission is more effective in terms of encouraging the ethical use of GenAI, due to students needing to explain how they utilise AI.

One of the key concerns about GenAI is its potential to undermine students as authors. When GenAI is used to complete assignments on behalf of students, it threatens to diminish the impact of the learning that comes with academic study. Being aware of this, I keep my work focused on learning and avoid the inclusion of artificial intelligence in this manner. The new course provides traffic lights guidance for better understanding what is ethical and what is not. This education on the limitations of artificial intelligence has discouraged me from over-relying on AI in my academic pursuits, encouraging me to use it as a tool rather than a substitute for my intellectual, scholarly work.

References

Abasi, A. and Graves, B. (2008) Academic literacy and plagiarism: Conversations with international graduate students and disciplinary professors. *Journal of English for Academic Purposes*, 7(4), pp. 221–233. Available at: https://doi.org/10.1016/j.jeap.2008.10.010.

Božić, V. (2023) Risks of digital divide in using artificial intelligence (AI). *Pre-print*. Available at: https://doi.org/10.13140/RG.2.2.18156.13443.

Brown, N. and Leigh, J. (Eds.) (2020) *Ableism in Academia: Theorising Experiences of Disabilities and Chronic Illnesses in Higher Education*. London: UCL Press. Available at: https://doi.org/10.14324/111.9781787354975.

CAST (2018) *Universal Design for Learning Guidelines (Version 2.2)*. Available at: http://udlguidelines.cast.org (Accessed 30 November 2023).

Christou, P.A. (2023) A critical perspective over whether and how to acknowledge the use of artificial intelligence (AI) in qualitative studies. *The Qualitative Report*, 28(7), pp. 1981–1991. Available at: https://doi.org/10.46743/2160-3715/2023.6407.

Davis, M. (2022) Examining and improving inclusive practice in institutional academic integrity policies, procedures, teaching and support. *International Journal for Educational Integrity*, 18(14) Available at: https://doi.org/10.1007/s40979-022-00108-x.

Davis, M. (2023) Inclusion within a holistic approach to academic integrity: Improving policy, pedagogy, and wider practice for all students. In Eaton, S.E. (Ed.), *Handbook of Academic Integrity*. Singapore: Springer. Available at: https://doi.org/10.1007/978-981-287-079-7_127-1.

Eaton, S.E. (2022) New priorities for academic integrity: Equity, diversity, inclusion, decolonization and Indigenization. *International Journal for Educational Integrity*, 18(10). Available at https://doi.org/10.1007/s40979-022-00105-0.

Eaton, S.E., Vogt, L., Seeland, J. and Stoesz, B.M. (2023) *Academic Integrity Policy Analysis of Alberta and Manitoba Colleges*. Canada: Canadian Symposium on Academic Integrity (CSAI), University of Manitoba. Available at: https://hdl.handle.net/1880/116575 (Accessed 30 November 2023).

Foltynek, T., Bjelobaba, S., Glendinning, I., Khan, Z.R., Santos, R., Pavletic, P. and Kravjar, J. (2023) ENAI recommendations on the ethical use of artificial intelligence in education. *International Journal for Educational Integrity*, 19(12). Available at: https://doi.org/10.1007/s40979-023-00133-4.

Illingsworth, S. (2023) If AI is to become a key tool in education, access has to be equal. *The Conversation*. Available at: https://theconversation.com/if-ai-is-to-become-a-key-tool-in-education-access-has-to-be-equal-204156#comment_2913535 (Accessed 30 November 2023).

Supporting inclusion in academic integrity in the age of GenAI 29

International Centre for Academic Integrity (ICAI) (2019) _Fundamental Values of Academic Integrity_, 3rd ed. Available at: https://academicintegrity.org/resources/fundamental-values (Accessed 30 November 2023).

Joint Information Statistics Committee (JISC) (2023) _Generative AI Primer_. National Centre for AI. Available at: https://nationalcentreforai.jiscinvolve.org/wp/2023/05/11/generative-ai-primer/ (Accessed 30 November 2023).

Kalejs, E. (2023) How AI can boost digital inclusion: Leaving no one behind or offline. _AI for Good_. Available at: https://aiforgood.itu.int/how-ai-can-boost-digital-inclusion-leaving-no-one-behind-or-offline/ (Accessed 30 November 2023).

Kaplan, S., and Ravanera, C. (2022) _An Equity Lens on Artificial Intelligence_. Social Sciences and Humanities Research Council in Collaboration with the Future Skills Centre. Available at: www.sshrc-crsh.gc.ca/society-societe/community-communite/ifcaiac/evidence_briefs-donnees_probantes/skills_work_digital_economy-competences_travail_economie_numerique/kaplan_ravaneraeng.aspx (Accessed 30 November 2023).

King's College London (2023) _Get Funding to Develop a Generative Artificial Intelligence Project_. Available at: www.kcl.ac.uk/students/get-funding-to-develop-a-generative-artificial-intelligence-ai-project (Accessed 2 December 2023).

Leask, B. (2006) Plagiarism, cultural diversity and metaphor – implications for academic staff development. _Assessment and Evaluation in Higher Education_, 31(2), pp. 183–199. Available at: https://doi.org/10.1080/02602930500262486.

Lynch, J., Salamonson, Y., Glew, P. and Ramjan, L. (2021) I'm not an investigator and I'm not a police officer – a faculty's view on academic integrity in an undergraduate nursing degree. _International Journal for Educational Integrity_, 17(19). Available at: https://doi.org/10.1007/s40979-021-00086-6.

McCormick, M. and Harvey, C. (2018) _The Traffic Lights Toolkit: A Guide for Practitioners in Higher Education_. Canterbury Christ Church University HEFCE. Available at: www.canterbury.ac.uk/learning-and-teaching-enhancement/docs/traffic-light-toolkit/The-Traffic-Lights-Toolkit-A-guide-for-practitioners-in-Higher-Education.pdf (Accessed 30 November 23).

Pecorari, D. and Shaw, P. (2012) Types of student intertextuality and faculty attitudes. _Journal of Second Language Writing_, 21, pp. 149–164. Available at: https://doi.org/10.1016/j.jslw.2012.03.006.

Sample Ward, A. and Bruce, A. (2023) _The Tech that Comes Next_. Hoboken, New Jersey: Wiley.

Thomas, L. and May, H. (2010) _Inclusive Learning and Teaching in Higher Education_. HE Academy. Available at: www.advance-he.ac.uk/knowledge-hub/inclusive-learning-and-teaching-higher-education (Accessed 30 November 2023).

United Nations Educational, Scientific and Cultural Organisation (UNESCO) (2023) _Guidance for Generative AI in Education and Research_. Available at: www.unesco.org/en/articles/guidance-generative-ai-education-and-research. (Accessed 30 November 2023).

Zajko, M. (2022) Artificial intelligence, algorithms, and social inequality: Sociological contributions to contemporary debates. _Sociology Compass_, 16(3), p. e12962. Available at: https://doi.org/10.1111/soc4.12962.

Part B

Developing generative AI literacies

4 Confidence enhancer, learning equalizer, and pedagogical ally

Exploring GenAI for students with English as an additional language

James Bedford, Mira Kim, and James Ciyu Qin

Introduction

This student–staff collaborative paper explores how generative artificial intelligence (GenAI) tools, such as ChatGPT, can be used to encourage learning and improve EAL students' confidence in writing and research-related tasks. Our study focuses on EAL students in an autonomous English learning context with an examination of one student's engagement with ChatGPT over two terms. Based on our extensive work with students in this area, we believe Qin's experiences are typical of other EAL students who are using these tools to improve their English language skills. Studies show that EAL students face many unique challenges in their university life, which can often impede or negatively impact their studies and their confidence (Ma, 2021). These challenges range from difficulty writing and speaking in English, to understanding academic writing conventions, and navigating student–supervisor communications. Qin's use of ChatGPT, which he implemented during the Personalised English Language Enhancement (*PELE*) course, demonstrates how GenAI tools might help students improve in these areas and be viewed as confidence enhancers, learning equalizers, and pedagogical allies.

As outlined in the literature review, the use of GenAI tools to support students in education comes with many challenges. As advanced as they are, these tools still lack the sophistication, nuance, and understanding of human beings, and, for that reason, we strongly encourage that programmes like ChatGPT do not act as a replacement for educational relationships. Instead, GenAI should complement and encourage further development of students' critical thinking, communication, and other key skills through continued guidance and support from human instructors. The goal should be to utilise GenAI as an additional resource for empowering and equipping students rather than allowing the technology to replace human insight and instruction.

DOI: 10.4324/9781003482918-6

In addition, while this paper aims to explore how GenAI can support autonomous learning, we recommend students are taught how to use and evaluate these tools effectively alongside teaching professionals and dedicated writing support staff. As part of the effective use of ChatGPT, in particular, students should develop their AI literacy, a term defined as:

> a set of competencies that enables individuals to critically evaluate AI technologies, communicate and collaborate effectively with AI, and use AI as a tool online, at home, and in the workplace.
>
> (Long and Magerko, 2020, p. 2)

Developing competency in this area will allow students to navigate the many risks involved in using such a powerful technology.

Literature review

There is plenty of research which has shown EAL students face many unique challenges in their university life. As a result, universities have often supported the diverse learning needs of EAL students with a number of services and interventions designed to assist the development of English language skills and academic literacy. These interventions range from academic skills services, writing workshops, thesis bootcamps, and embedded language and learning support (Briguglio and Watson, 2014). The challenge these support services often face is scalability, or difficulty providing quality assistance to a high number of students at regular stages of their research and writing process.

The increasing use of GenAI by English as Additional Language (EAL) students brings not only a number of challenges but also opportunities to those students wanting to improve their English language skills. Some concerns are that prolonged use of tools like ChatGPT may decrease higher-order thinking skills over time, such as critical thinking (Putra et al., 2023). Other concerns are that students might use these tools to submit work that is not their own, increasing the likelihood of cheating (Perkins, 2023). In addition, there is the risk of bias and misinformation in the output these tools provide (Borenstein and Howard, 2021). There is also the issue of privacy and data collection, whereby responses submitted to these tools might be used as training materials for future outputs (Borenstein and Howard, 2021; Khowaja et al., 2023). There is also the issue of hallucinations, defined as '[the] making up of plausible material' (Mollick and Mollick, 2023) which presents a unique challenge to the accuracy of information these tools provide.

It is noteworthy, however, that the benefits of GenAI for student learning are as profound as the ethical challenges it poses. Some studies have suggested that there are multiple roles a large language model like ChatGPT could play in a student's learning, ranging from AI merely offloading cognitive work, to

AI being more deeply integrated and collaborating within the learning process through co-regulation and hybrid learning partnerships (Lodge et al., 2023). GenAI's ability to give students instant and personalised feedback on their writing and research tasks is also very alluring (Kasneci et al., 2023). LLMs can also be used by students to help clarify difficult concepts or ideas they are struggling to understand (Kasneci et al., 2023). In addition, with its multilingual capabilities, GenAI tools can provide support to students in all types of languages.

GenAI could profoundly improve education by enhancing teaching and learning practices while empowering teachers and students. These tools may enable personalised, engaging instruction and provide extra support for learners. However, realising the full potential of GenAI tools requires deep collaborative efforts to address the many risks involved. For this reason, it is recommended that EAL students engaging with LLMs to support their studies should be guided by the educational approach of autonomous learning. Autonomous learning encourages self-directed and independent work, whereby learners take responsibility for their educational experiences and use a variety of resources in the process. In pedagogical terms, autonomous learning requires scaffolding learning activities, training students in strategies for planning and monitoring their progress, and explicit reflection mechanisms to develop metacognitive awareness (Cotterall, 2000). GenAI tools will offer a supportive resource that could greatly enhance a student's capacity for independent learning, though students need to be able to take ownership and responsibility for their own ethical use of these tools. While receiving guidance from instructors and institutions to understand the limitations and potential pitfalls involved, students should be equipped to leverage GenAI responsibly to enrich their learning experience.

Context of research

Personalised English Language Enhancement (PELE) is a 10-week long credit-bearing course designed to support EAL students to enhance their English Language Proficiency. It offers a holistic approach based on a personalised autonomous (PA) model that guides students to personalise their own learning journey through a series of steps that include analysing their communication context; identifying linguistic needs; designing a personal project; implementing the project; and reflecting on their progress. Research has shown significant impacts of the approach on students' confidence, self-efficacy, motivation, engagement, and sense of belonging (Kim, 2023).

Since this course aims to assist EAL students to further enhance their abilities in communicating in English, it offers an ideal opportunity to examine how learners utilise GenAI tools to enhance their academic skills and English proficiency. In the following section, we present a case study of the student,

Qin, who used ChatGPT as a learning tool to support his academic studies over the programme, doing so in order to determine whether ChatGPT helped improve his confidence, writing ability, and overall academic performance.

Qin's case

Qin, a PhD student from China, began his English education in kindergarten, a pursuit shaped by his parents' aspirations for his international schooling. Recognised for his linguistic talent, he led reading sessions and was the voice of the school's English broadcasts in his seventh grade. His proficiency secured him a place in an international high school, skipping a year to advance his studies. During his university education in mechanical and manufacturing engineering, Qin confronted unexpected challenges, particularly in writing and presenting for design courses. This revealed a gap between his and native English speakers' writing skills and led to a sense of insecurity. His confidence continued to wane in his honours year after receiving unclear and slightly critical feedback on his literature review, in addition to a lack of quality feedback from his supervisor.

When his application for a PhD was approved, he started to gain back some of his confidence. However, Qin's morale was quickly undermined by journal rejections and ambiguous advice on his writing, leaving him feeling lost and questioning his path. Qin decided to enrol in the PELE course to find ways of improving his English. He soon found this was a challenging task, even after utilising diagnostic questionnaires, vocabulary tests, and self-evaluation. He understood his most important priority was to improve his academic writing skills for his thesis, but he was unsure which aspects needed the most attention – whether it was the writing structure, the choice of words, or the writing style in general. Previously, he had received feedback that had likened his work to a 'high school report' or 'not like a journal paper'. This was not very helpful and, to a certain degree, made him feel even more confused. These sorts of comments are not uncommon for EAL students who receive feedback that doesn't address the issues with their language or expression nor identify ways of resolving these issues. It was nonetheless surprising that such remarks would suffice as 'feedback' in a higher education setting. In response, Qin decided to examine the linguistic concepts of writing that had been introduced during the PELE lectures and worked hard to develop and improve his English in this programme.

Since his PELE tutor had introduced the latest technology trend of GenAI, he was able to use ChatGPT as an additional tool to better understand linguistic concepts and to develop his work. This was an eye-opening experience which eventually led him to realise (based on suggestions provided by ChatGPT) that what may be impeding his writing was text structure, nominalisation, and academic productive vocabulary. He found AI-assisted learning was a more efficient way for him to identify these issues in his writing and began to ask ChatGPT for more related examples and detailed explanations of these linguistic concepts. As a result, he started to feel more secure in his writing ability because he had, at the very least, an idea of what he might need to work on.

He then designed a personal project to enhance his academic writing skills, specifically with the goal being to create a literature review chapter with a higher degree of complexity and nuance. Qin wanted to be capable of writing in a way that was both formal and critical, as well as being understandable and accessible to the reader. He aimed to achieve this by focusing on the concepts of formal academic vocabulary, paragraph coherence and cohesion, and nominalisation. To find relevant academic vocabulary, he recorded new words while reading literature, and he practised paragraph coherence and cohesion, as well as nominalisation throughout his thesis writing journey. GenAI played an important role in this process, particularly as a tutor to teach him new words he had recorded. Since his goal was to expand productive vocabulary, simply knowing the meaning of a new word was not enough. With GenAI, he was able to receive tailored questions, examples, and even quizzes to help him better understand and practice his expanding vocabulary.

With the assistance of GenAI, Qin's approach to writing has greatly transformed. By functioning as an available, personalised tutor or assistant, GenAI earned an ally status – working collaboratively with Qin throughout the writing process. In this case, the pedagogical dimension surfaces through an ally that teaches, as opposed to doing the work for him. Qin's expanded vocabulary and understanding of paragraph cohesion, a direct result of his diligent learning and GenAI's guidance, has not only improved his writing quality but also reignited his passion for writing.

Discussion

Qin's engagement with ChatGPT to support his studies had many positive outcomes. For example, his ability to engage in a back-and-forth dialogue proved particularly useful as he was able to ask for further clarification or examples when needed. He also found the suggestions provided by GenAI followed a praise–criticism–praise structure, which not only gave him useful suggestions for improving his work but boosted his motivation to write. Importantly, engaging with GenAI tools in the writing and research process alleviated many of his procrastination tendencies, enabling him to focus more on content creation and the exploration of new ideas and perspectives. In addition, when submitting his work, Qin felt more confident, knowing that his writing had undergone some preliminary review.

This is important given EAL students often lose confidence when markers provide feedback that focuses on typo errors and issues with expression rather than providing more comprehensive and helpful advice. Lee's research shows when teachers devote time to correcting grammatical or linguistic errors in an EAL student's written work, it is often more problematic for the students receiving the feedback (Lee, 2019). This is because corrective, error-focused feedback often places too much emphasis on minor grammatical mistakes rather than on meaning and communication. Such corrective feedback can undermine students' confidence, which is a key motivator to continue writing and improving one's work. Given many educators are not formally trained to advise students on their written English language and speaking skills, allowing students to use programmes like ChatGPT for editing and refining text could improve the quality of feedback EAL students receive from their teachers.

Based on our work with EAL students, we have found that Qin's experience is akin to the experience of others using these tools. It is evident in Qin's case that he is now more confident in his writing abilities after using ChatGPT to support his studies and that he was able to improve in the areas he had identified after engaging with this tool. It is important to note, however, that Qin was not always fully satisfied with the outputs ChatGPT provided. In some cases, ChatGPT's suggestions were incorrect or unhelpful. When the use of GenAI resulted in any uncertainty or confusion, Qin sought professional guidance from English language support experts at his university. We recommend other students do the same.

Qin's experience shows how GenAI has excellent potential in promoting learner autonomy. The technology empowered Qin to take more initiative over his learning: identifying key problem areas in his writing, receiving customised help from ChatGPT to deepen his understanding of concepts, designing a personal project to strengthen skills, and using the AI as an ally and a tutor to enrich his productive vocabulary. However, the case also indicates risks if students solely rely on generative models without sufficient support. Despite ChatGPT offering helpful explanations, Qin still required human educators to actually diagnose the issues in his writing and point him in the right direction.

Conclusion

In many ways, using GenAI tools has become a new academic skill, one that many students will need to develop as part of their education. While we do not wish to promote the widespread use of these tools in all given contexts, we have attempted to examine effective and appropriate use cases in certain settings, while allowing students to have their say about how these tools are impacting and supporting their studies. It is hoped our discussion supports educational leaders to make informed and critical decisions about the role GenAI plays in higher education, as well as provide a better understanding of its abilities and limitations in assisting students throughout the learning process. Undoubtedly, the presence of tools like ChatGPT in education will require a deep consideration of both the challenges and potential benefits. However, when used ethically and responsibly, GenAI can serve as a confidence enhancer, learning equalizer, and pedagogical ally, providing an additional space for students to develop their skills in an autonomous learning environment.

Evaluation

Serena Wei Sun, PhD candidate and mentor, UNSW

I've been involved in evaluating the practices outlined in the chapter/case study through my experience mentoring students who utilised AI tools in their coursework like PELE.

What I found particularly interesting and valuable about the outlined practices was the integration of GenAI literature and the PELE practice into higher education. The utilisation of AI tools not only enhances learning experiences but also encourages innovative thinking and creativity among students.

From the practices outlined, I learned the significance of incorporating AI technology to augment traditional educational methods. GenAI enables the creation of adaptive environments that cater to individual student needs, which provides a tailored learning experience for each student. The integration of AI tools, as showcased in this project, has inspired me to explore similar approaches in other educational settings, fostering an enriched educational experience that transcends traditional boundaries and recognising the potential to improve student engagement and critical thinking skills.

This collaborative effort between James Bedford, James Qin, and Mira Kim provides an insightful perspective on leveraging AI in higher education, paving the way for a more adaptive and interactive learning environment. Additionally, in this chapter, I was reminded how crucial it is to utilise these tools responsibly within ethical boundaries, ensuring that they serve as a tool for assistance rather than being subject to misuse.

References

Borenstein, J. and Howard, A. (2021) Emerging challenges in AI and the need for AI ethics education. *AI and Ethics*, 1, pp. 61–65 Available at: https://doi.org/10.1007/s43681-020-00002-7 (Accessed 26 January 2024).

Briguglio, C. and Watson, S. (2014) Embedding English language across the curriculum in higher education: A continuum of development support. *Australian Journal of Language and Literacy*, 37, pp. 67–74. Available at: https://doi.org/10.1007/BF03651933 (Accessed 26 January 2024).

Cotterall, S. (2000) Promoting learner autonomy through the curriculum: Principles for designing language courses. *ELT Journal*, 54(2), pp. 109–117. Oxford University Press. Available at: https://doi.org/10.1093/elt/54.2.109 (Accessed 26 January 2024).

Cotton, D.R.E., Cotton, P.A. and Shipway, J.R. (2023) Chatting and cheating: Ensuring academic integrity in the era of ChatGPT. *Innovations in Education and Teaching International*. Available at: https://doi.org/10.1080/1470 3297.2023.2190148 (Accessed 26 January 2024).

Kasneci, E., Sessler, K., Küchemann, S., Bannert, M., Dementieva, D., Fischer, F., Gasser, U., Groh, G., Günnemann, S., Hüllermeier, E., Krusche, S., Kutyniok, G., Michaeli, T., Nerdel, C., Pfeffer, J., Poquet, O., Sailer, M., Schmidt, A., Seidel, T., Stadler, M., Weller, J., Kuhn, J. and Kasneci, G. (2023) ChatGPT for good? On opportunities and challenges of large language models for education. *Learning and Individual Differences*, 103, pp. 1–19. Available at: https://doi.org/10.1016/j.lindif.2023.102274 (Accessed 26 January 2024).

Khowaja, S.A., Khuwaja, P. and Dev, K. (2023) ChatGPT needs SPADE (sustainability, privacy, digital divide, and ethics) evaluation: A review. *Computers and Society*. Available at: https://arxiv.org/abs/2305.03123 (Accessed 26 January 2024).

Kim, M. (2023) A personalised autonomous model to resolve a prolonged dilemma in international students' English language needs in higher education. *Higher Education Research & Development*, 42(3), pp. 603–618. Available at: https://doi.org/10.1080/07294360.2022.2105823 (Accessed 26 January 2024).

Lee, I. (2019) Teacher written corrective feedback: Less is more. *Language Teaching*, 52(4), pp. 524–536. Cambridge University Press. Available at: https://doi.org/10.1017/S0261444819000247 (Accessed 26 January 2024).

Lodge, J.M., Yang, S., Furze, L. and Dawson, P. (2023) It's not like a calculator, so what is the relationship between learners and generative artificial intelligence? *Learning: Research and Practice*, 9(2), pp. 117–124. Available at: https://doi.org/10.1080/23735082.2023.2261106 (Accessed 26 January 2024).

Long, D. and Magerko, B. (2020) 'What is AI literacy? Competencies and design considerations. In *Proceedings of the 2020 CHI Conference on Human Factors in Computing Systems (CHI '20)*. Association for Computing Machinery, New York, NY, USA, pp. 1–16. Available at: https://doi.org/10.1145/3313831.3376727 (Accessed 26 January 2024).

Ma, L. (2021) Writing in English as an additional language: Challenges encountered by doctoral students. *Higher Education Research & Development*, 40(6), pp. 1176–1190. Available at: https://doi.org/10.1080/07294360. 2020.1809354 (Accessed 26 January 2024).

Mollick, E.R. and Mollick, L. (2023) *Using AI to Implement Effective Teaching Strategies in Classrooms: Five Strategies, Including Prompts*. Available at: https://doi.org/10.2139/ssrn.4391243 (Accessed 26 January 2024).

Perkins, M. (2023) Academic integrity considerations of AI large language models in the post-pandemic era: ChatGPT and beyond. *Journal of*

University Teaching & Learning Practice, 20(2). Available at: https://doi.
org/ 10.53761/1.20.02.07 (Accessed 26 January 2024).

Putra, F.W., Rangka, I.B., Aminah, S. and Aditama, M.H.R. (2023) ChatGPT
in the higher education environment: Perspectives from the theory of high
order thinking skills. *Journal of Public Health*. Available at: https://doi.
org/10.1093/pubmed/fdad120 (Accessed 26 January 2024).

5 Integrating GenAI in higher education

Insights, perceptions, and a taxonomy of practice

*Samantha Newell, Rachel Fitzgerald,
Kimberley Hall, Jennie Mills, Tina Beynen,
Ivy Chia Sook May, Jon Mason,
and Evelyn Lai*

Introduction

Generative artificial intelligence (GenAI) offers new possibilities for person-alised learning experiences (Escotet, 2023) but the fast-paced evolution of GenAI (Fowler, 2023) has led to both resistance and experimentation among educators (Eager and Brunton, 2023; Newell, 2023). Educator attitudes and approaches to integrating GenAI into practice vary widely. The scale and scope of variation are significant and worthy of scholarly exploration as are the attitudes, beliefs, and experiences of educators that will shape future educational practice. This chapter provides insights into fears about GenAI, and expectations and emerging practices from educators worldwide. We examine whether experiences from GenAI integration can mitigate educational disparities, to position GenAI as a 'beneficial disruptor' in higher education (HE) (Powell et al., 2015). By delineating emerging patterns from current use, this chapter guides educators on the relationship between values and practice, perceptions about the ethics of GenAI (UNESCO, 2021b), and the use of GenAI for 'common good' (Sabzalieva and Valentini, 2023).

There is intrinsic value in this 'snapshot' of practice which captures GenAI/HE discourse. Practitioners will recognise many of the attitudes outlined here and be able to situate their own position within it. There is also value in considering how the discourse evolves, and how encounters and dialogue shape understanding and behaviour. We offer an opportunity to reflect upon the dialogic and community nature of innovation as a process – and to consider our role as educators in creating and sustaining the conditions within which pedagogical innovation can flourish.

We collected publicly available 'open data' posts (Quinn, 2020) during July 2023, from a large, open Facebook (FB) group, where educators from HE discuss implications of GenAI for their teaching practice. The group

DOI: 10.4324/9781003482918-7

comprises 3,600 members, increasing by around 200 members each week (in November 2023), a highly active group with ~13 new posts/day.

As an international group of researchers engaged in digital education at different institutions, we drew upon our distinct experiences and contexts to find an analytical approach. Three theoretical lenses that connected with the discourse and context were foregrounded: the Diffusion of Innovations theory (DOI) (Rogers, 2003), Fawns' 'entangled pedagogy' (2022), and Bourdieu's social capital theory (1986). While each of the three theories provides unique perspectives on GenAI, we expected benefits from their integration. They help clarify the understanding of GenAI among educators and offer insights into teaching, learning, and the social dynamics within HE. More importantly, these context-agnostic theories can be applied to various contexts across the educational landscape.

In analysing the posts through qualitative content analysis (QCA) (Schreier, 2012), we developed a values-based taxonomy of practice (p. 47). As educators' values appeared to shape behaviours and decision-making, a taxonomy of practice helps clarify the relationship between values and action.

GenAI: Adoption or perception of value?

The five-stage model that is Rogers' Diffusion of Innovations (DOI) theory (2003) broadly groups technology users into 'innovators', 'early adopters', and 'laggards' (Rogers, 2003).

In this model, individuals seek and process information to reduce uncertainty and to determine the relative advantages and/or disadvantages of the [technical] innovation. Using this model to consider individual educators' innovation-decision process, most educators were at the persuasion stage.

Educators' conversations implied that the adoption of GenAI may not be as swift, uniform, or complete as predicted. Their comments also suggested that educator understanding about student values and behaviours impacts their perceptions of GenAI and its potential.

An overarching theme was that integrating GenAI into HE is more of a burden than a boon. Fast-paced development, inherent untrustworthiness, and

Figure 5.1 Rogers' (2003) 'Diffusion of Innovation' five-stage model. Adapted from Rogers' (2003).

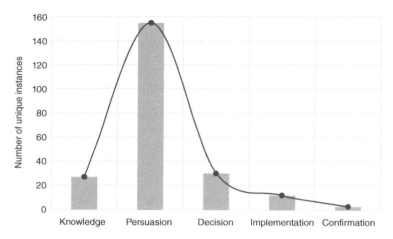

Figure 5.2 Facebook discussions mapped against the Diffusion of Innovations categories (Rogers, 2003).

inaccurate output require additional time for verification (negating any perceived time saving). There was also a sense that GenAI diminishes student engagement, hinders learning, and impacts performance. More positively, administrative tasks, such as building websites, day-to-day communication, and ideas generation for learning activities, were considered areas where GenAI could be beneficial. Strikingly, there were no conversations about how difficult GenAI is to use. Ease of use and individual educator autonomy fosters an atmosphere of experimentation and a mindset of 'let's see what it can do'. Technological complexity is not a barrier to adoption.

Rogers' (2003) suggests that the 'decision' stage is where individuals determine whether to adopt a new technology. However, the Facebook data found most educators lingering in the 'persuasion' stage. The prolonged state of 'persuasion' indicates how the entwined discussion of values and practice can facilitate productive conversations about decision-making in HE institutions. This discursive snapshot exemplifies how the characterisation of GenAI within the HE social system directly impacts on how far, fast, or how well GenAI creates pedagogic change. Presenting the perceptions of educators at an early stage of decision-making offers a way to consider future practice. That so many educators were in the persuasion phase suggests that the model requires more nuance in terms of understanding what is persuading/dissuading. Similarly, how educators' values influence 'decision', 'implementation', and subsequent adoption needs further consideration.

A complex consideration of utility and potential harm

While aligning with some pedagogic practices, many educators considered GenAI incompatible with their perception of student practice and values, characterised in the posts as

- instrumental approaches to study,
- preoccupation with career goals, and
- predisposition to cheat.

Many pedagogic innovations (including GenAI) are informed by a student-deficit model, particularly academic dishonesty. In this respect, educators believed students were further along in their GenAI innovation/decision-making process than they are.

The belief that 'GenAI harms learning' was coupled with a certainty that most students perceive only advantages in its' use. This narrative uncharitably depicts students as indifferent/unaware of learning as an intrinsic good. There was palpable anxiety and frustration (sometimes tipping into anger) that by interrupting the learning process, GenAI ultimately fails students. Some educators argued that the relative weakness of GenAI academic outputs (e.g. bland writing, poor referencing, and third-class criticality) affords 'teachable moments', supporting students to develop mastery of these essential skills.

Broader societal impact of AI

Ethical concerns were a significant focus, reflecting more widespread alarm. While 'AI literacy' lacks clear consensus (Ng et al., 2021), some educators teach students GenAI 'literacy' through critiquing GenAI outputs and comparing human/GenAI-generated feedback. Educators are dissuading students from relying on GenAI and some are re-evaluating written assessments by prioritising analysis/interpretation over content generation. This signifies a pedagogical shift. Others maintain traditional values yet meet the challenge through assessment methods like presentations and interactive orals (Newell, 2023). The move to explore ethical implications of GenAI in 'human' creative tasks emphasises the importance of teaching critical thinking skills alongside GenAI use.

The irreplaceable qualities of human intelligence, creativity, and students' unique contributions alongside GenAI are emphasised in the data. The ethical use of AI should 'empower students and teachers and enhance their experience' (UNESCO, 2021a, p. 34). Critical thinking about GenAI is intrinsically multi-disciplinary and requires students to discuss ethical and civic responsibility. This approach aligns with 'entangled pedagogy' (Fawns, 2022) and highlights the need for educators to theorise beyond pedagogy.

The reinvention of (higher) education and academic roles and responsibilities

Concerns that GenAI will initiate radical transformation of every aspect of practice were prevalent (including the rationale and mechanisms of assessment). From a student equity perspective, if access to GenAI is not standardised, then existing *digital divides* may be deepened, increasing educational disparity and diverging from sustainable education goals (UNESCO, 2021a). Educators expressed concern that ubiquitous GenAI use could worsen class disparities, resulting in lost cultural capital for certain groups. However, contributors also recognised the potential benefits to their personal social capital within networks that 'provides each member with collectively owned capital' (Bourdieu, 1986, p. 23), for example, resource sharing, or enhancing their professional image on platforms like LinkedIn. Curiosity surrounded ideas of replacing essential educator duties and the potential impact on reputation and staff equity, for example, comparing comprehensive feedback from trained instructors with more efficient (yet less-detailed) feedback from GenAI. In the Facebook group, these changes were often framed as losses in social or cultural capital for both instructors and students (Bourdieu, 1986).

Throughout Facebook discussions, educators sought to maintain academic values and commit to ethical/responsible use of GenAI with students. Values are driving decisions and are perceived to be threatened by GenAI. This is a call for an open discussion about values-driven pedagogy.

Reviewing values to consider a taxonomy of practice

More broadly, the FB group discussed how GenAI threatens fundamental purpose and values underpinning HE and adds to workload. Scepticism and frustration are common reactions to the novel practices outlined in the taxonomy. What is striking is that GenAI has already shifted the conversation and is challenging the orthodoxies of HE. Previous consensus on what constitutes 'good' and 'bad' practice in HE and boundaries between progressive and traditional pedagogy have become fuzzy.

Taxonomy of practice – values aligned with practice

The quadrants in Figure 5.3 indicate alternate values-driven pedagogical responses to GenAI integration, as explained below.

Shifting values to align with GenAI: Wholesale shift in practice

Several educators are re-evaluating the value of HE through GenAI, redefining 'essential skills' and questioning traditional academic tasks. These educators

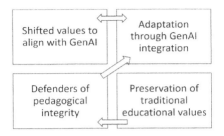

Figure 5.3 Taxonomy of values. Quadrants indicate alternate values-driven pedagogical responses to GenAI integration.

view GenAI as genuine co-production driven by human agency, not an 'us-versus-the-machines' scenario. Further classification includes the following.

Personalised learning

GenAI is valued as a catalyst for educational innovation. It can enhance teaching and learning without compromising quality (Escotet, 2023).

Challenging perceptions of a lack of 'humanness' with AI-augmenting empathy

A few educators utilise GenAI to augment their empathetic responses to students. GenAI is used to increase supportive language in feedback, in the context of rising academic burnout. GenAI's ability to simulate empathy challenges the beliefs of those designing assessments to avoid its use. Educators encourage students to question benchmarks like the Turing Test, to consider alternative ways of assessing AI-intelligence.

Adaptation through GenAI integration: Not a paradigm shift, but can it help me reach my existing goals?

Educators are open to adapting teaching methods, seeking ways to align GenAI with their core educational values, including the following.

Student-centred learning

They believed that GenAI could tailor education to individual student needs, foster a more personalised learning experience. Alongside this is a shift in practice towards what constitutes 'authentic assessment', as discussed in Bearman et al. (2023).

Accessibility

Accessible education is valued and GenAI is perceived as removing barriers and enhancing resource access.

Defenders of pedagogical integrity: Deterring students using 'shortcuts'

Educators prioritised pedagogical integrity, including the following.

Concerns that GenAI will increase shallow learning

They value authentic learning experiences where students actively engage with course content, demonstrate their understanding, and apply knowledge in real-world contexts.

Academic honesty

They expressed concerns that GenAI could facilitate academic dishonesty and aim to prevent it.

Concerned that students will not achieve learning outcomes

They focus on students developing subject matter expertise – concerns associated with outsourcing text generation. If students do not write the text, then they are unlikely to be thinking about it.

Preservation of traditional educational values

Educators seek to preserve traditional values in HE, including the following.

Human-centric education

They believe education is fundamentally about the personal interaction between educators and students, valuing face-to-face teaching, mentorship, agency, and the human touch in the learning process.

Scepticism of technology

They are sceptical of technology's role in education, reifying traditional/non-digital teaching methods and in-person interactions as fundamental.

Educators not interested in teaching AI

They prioritise their core pedagogical roles and subject expertise over teaching GenAI, focusing on developing writing skills rather than supporting GenAI usage. They see no benefit to students by integrating GenAI into student workflow.

A taxonomy for change management

The taxonomy can be utilised by communities of practice or academic developers. The taxonomy helps align individual values with institutional goals, fostering consistency of practice, allowing ethical decision-making by different parties, and easing through institutional change. For example, at the leadership level, the taxonomy allows leaders to initiate discussions about educators' values, particularly as any push for institutions to integrate GenAI into the curriculum may challenge such values.

A community dedicated to sharing experiences may persuade educators not interested in teaching GenAI (in terms of perceived additional workload, or the perceived lack of benefit to students). Educators can also pinpoint common challenges, uncertainties, and work-in-progress. Articulating boundaries (and when they believe others' boundaries to be misplaced) can give rise to a shared imperative as a 'we' emerges. Through intentional, and evidence-led discussions (framed around the taxonomy), we provide an avenue for HE leaders to address points of tension in relation to the values-practice nexus.

Is the genie out of the bottle?
The implications of GenAI on future practice

GenAI has the power to be the ultimate disruptive innovation (Christensen et al., 2015). In our analysis of educator discussions, we observed that GenAI is impacting pedagogical design, assessment, academic integrity, and the purpose of HE. In July 2023, there was very little GenAI 'adoption' and many educators were fluctuating between the persuasion and decision stages of adoption. It is highly possible that given the pace of technological innovation, this flux will become the norm. Understanding the values/concerns motivating this prolonged decision period allows leaders to adequately shape practice and policy to address this stage of innovation adoption in three ways.

Institutional policy and practice

The importance of providing educators with time and opportunities to learn about GenAI and rethink curriculum and assessment was a critical theme.

This implies that contributors to the Facebook discussion are concerned about their less-informed colleagues. We suggest this is an area of focus for future policy/practice within our institutions.

Management response to perceiving GenAI as a disruption plays a decisive role in HE's future. We need to consider governance regarding processes, systems, and working practices and provide clarity on institutional policy. It is also inevitable that timely GenAI training is required for many educators and, for many, this may include a need for a broader understanding of pedagogy (Sankey et al., 2023).

The taxonomy of practice we developed is a good starting point for discussion, especially in aligning the values of individual educators with institutional goals, examining current practice and locating opportunities and stages of professional development for staff, alongside creating GenAI policies (discussed below).

Equitable policies and training for faculty

Not all educators have time/resources for comprehensive GenAI training. Such a requirement for professional development is not surprising and has been well documented since the early days of the digital revolution (Abdal-Haqq, 1996; Hennessy et al., 2022). Similarly, organisations have encountered a need for 'adoption and integration' in the context of digital transformation, leading to various 'maturity models' (Ifenthaler and Egloffstein, 2020). There is a pressing need for staff policies and training encompassing all faculty members, including casual tutors and sessional academics, addressing GenAI use in grading and feedback.

Crafting explicit GenAI policies for students

Educators from the Facebook group emphasise the importance of ethical use by encouraging students to acknowledge the source of GenAI-generated content (and cite GenAI appropriately). Others develop policies against using GenAI for original thought in assignments. New guidelines can be constructed alongside policy recommendations outlined in UNESCO (2021a, 2021b). There is a need for continual discussion and engagement.

Conclusion

In general, educators emphasise the importance of teaching critical thinking and writing skills, even where GenAI can assist with various aspects of writing. Many are concerned about the shortcuts it offers students, yet express commitment to teaching students how to use GenAI ethically and responsibly.

There is confidence that GenAI should complement, not replace, human creativity and engagement. Educators are keen on ensuring that students are not only users but also informed evaluators of AI. They want students to recognise the limitations of GenAI, particularly in judgment and values.

What is next for higher education?

While HE institutions are often seen as slow to adapt to change and disruptive innovation (Powell et al., 2015), COVID-19 demonstrated their ability to respond on a large scale. HE has proven its adaptability in the face of disruption, even with short notice (Fitzgerald et al., 2023) and GenAI provides educators with an opportunity to get creative in rethinking education (Rapanta et al., 2021). This assures us that GenAI will contribute to the evolution of HE, rather than being a destroyer. However, there is enough uncertainty in how it will contribute that we must ensure that we stick to values-based and evidence-informed practice and keep our HE communities connected as we progress in an uncertain world.

Creating space for a discussion about values

This chapter was based on a snapshot in time, but the conversation has not changed; we believe this taxonomy of practice will guide our thinking. Educator values are still underpinning changes to practice regarding GenAI integration. Addressing the values outlined in the taxonomy can facilitate dialogue and reflection among educators, promoting a better understanding of GenAI's benefits and challenges, as well as setting direction in decision-making within institutions and communities of practice. This approach encourages constructive conversations with sceptical staff, fostering an inclusive and informed transition aligned with the evolving educational landscape.

Critical evaluation

Dr Beate Brunow, Educational Developer and Associate Director of the Schreyer Institute for Teaching Excellence, Pennsylvania State University, USA
    An analysis of open data from a large educator Facebook group offers an insightful snapshot in July 2023 of educator sentiments, practices, and experiences regarding GenAI. GenAI has already proven to be a significant disruptor in HE as it challenges instructors and institutions to reconsider the purpose of HE and to contend with the values and ethics that underlie our missions and objectives. Educators approach GenAI and its impact on all aspects of teaching – from course design and delivery to assessment of student learning – based on their values, and the authors propose an emerging taxonomy of

practice that reflects the alignment of values and practice. To support change along the taxonomy, institutions need to provide opportunities for critical and comprehensive discussions about the role of GenAI and educators' values (e.g. what is the purpose of teaching a certain topic or skill) and beliefs (e.g. how students learn) that guide their practice. In addition, access to professional development appears equally important to ensure equitable integration. GenAI might demand that we centre students in our conversations about ethics and the roles and values of HE and take a closer look at current pedagogical practices and how they intersect with the lives of learners and their paths after graduation. In that way, the arrival of GenAI in HE might contribute to the evolution of higher education.

References

Abdal-Haqq, I. (1996) *Making Time for Teacher Professional Development.* ERIC Digest. Available at: https://files.eric.ed.gov/fulltext/ED400259.pdf (Accessed 26 January 2024).

Bearman, M., Ajjawi, R., Boud, D., Tai, J. and Dawson, P. (2023) *CRADLE-Suggests: Assessment and GenAI. Centre for Research in Assessment and Digital Learning.* Australia: Deakin University. Available at: https://doi.org/10.6084/m9.figshare.22494178 (Accessed 26 January 2024).

Bourdieu, P. (1986) The forms of capital. In Richardson, J. (Ed.), *Handbook of Theory and Research for the Sociology of Education.* New York: Greenwood Press, pp. 241–225.

Christensen, C., Raynor, M.E. and McDonald, R. (2015) Disruptive innovation. *Harvard Business Review.* Available at: www.innosight.com/wp-content/uploads/2018/01/Innosight_HBR_What-is-Disruptive-Innovation.pdf.

Eager, B. and Brunton, R. (2023) Prompting higher education towards AI-augmented-teaching. *Journal of University Teaching and Learning Practice,* 20(5). Available at: https://doi.org/10.53761/1.20.5.02 (Accessed 26 January 2024).

Escotet, M.Á. (2023) *The Optimistic Future of Artificial-Intelligence in Higher-Education.* Springer. Available at: https://doi.org/10.1007/s11125-023-09642-z (Accessed 26 January 2024).

Fawns, T. (2022) An entangled pedagogy: Looking beyond the pedagogy-technology dichotomy. *Postdigital Science and Education,* 4(3), pp. 711–728. Available at: https://doi.org/10.1007/s42438-022-00302-7 (Accessed 26 January 2024).

Fitzgerald, R., Huijser, H., Altena, S. and Armellini, A. (2023) Addressing the challenging elements of distance-education. *Distance Education,* 44(2), pp. 207–212. Available at: https://doi.org/10.1080/01587919.2023.2209527 (Accessed 26 January 2024).

Fowler, G. (2023) We tested a new ChatGPT-detector for teachers. *Washington Post.* Washington, DC. Available at: www.washingtonpost.com/technology/2023/04/01/chatgpt-cheating-detection-turnitin/ (Accessed 15 July 2023).

Hennessy, S., D'Angelo, S., McIntyre, N., Koomar, S., Kreimeia, A., Cao, L., Brugha, M. and Zubairi, A. (2022) Technology use for teacher professional development in low-and middle-income countries: A systematic review. *Computers and Education*, 3. Available at: https://doi.org/10.1016/j.caeo.2022.100080.

Ifenthaler, D. and Egloffstein, M. (2020) Development and implementation of a maturity model of digital transformation. *TechTrends*, 64(2), pp. 302–309 Available at: https://doi.org/10.1007/s11528-019-00457-4 (Accessed 26 January 2024).

Newell, S. (2023) Employing the interactive oral to mitigate threats to academic integrity from ChatGPT. *Scholarship of Teaching and Learning in Psychology*. https://doi.org/10.1037/stl0000371.

Ng, D.T.K., Leung, J.K.L., Chu, K.W.S. and Qiao, M.S. (2021) AI literacy: Definition, teaching, evaluation and ethical issues. *Proceedings of the ASIST Annual Meeting*, 58(1), pp. 504–509. Available at: https://doi.org/10.1002/pra2.487 (Accessed 26 January 2024).

Powell, S., Olivier, B. and Yuan, L. (2015) Handling disruptive innovations in HE: Lessons from two contrasting case studies. *Research in Learning Technology*, 23. Available at: https://doi.org/10.3402/rlt.v23.22494 (Accessed 26 January 2024).

Quinn, F.F. (2020) The use of Facebook and other social media platforms in social science research. *SAGE Research Methods*. Available at: https://doi.org/10.4135/9781529700176 (Accessed 26 January 2024).

Rapanta, C., Botturi, L. and Goodyear, P. (2021) Balancing technology, pedagogy and the new normal: Post-pandemic challenges for HE. *Postdigital Science and Education*, 3, pp. 715–742. Available at: https://doi.org/10.1007/s42438-021-00249-1 (Accessed 26 January 2024).

Rogers, E.M. (2003) *Diffusion of Innovations*, 5th ed. New York: Free Press.

Sabzalieva, E. and Valentini, A. (2023) *ChatGPT and Artificial Intelligence in HE*. UNESCO. Available at: https://etico.iiep.unesco.org/en/chatgpt-and-artificial-intelligence-higher-education-quick-start-guide (Accessed 26 January 2024).

Sankey, M.D., Huijser, H. and Fitzgerald, R. (2023) The virtual university: Moving from fiction to fact. In Sankey, M.D., Huijser, H. and Fitzgerald, R. (Eds.), *Technology-Enhanced Learning and the Virtual University*. University Development and Administration, Springer. Available at: https://doi.org/10.1007/978-981-19-9438-8_1-1 (Accessed 26 January 2024).

Schreier, M. (2012) *Qualitative Content Analysis in Practice*. London: SAGE.

UNESCO (2021a) *AI and Education: Guidance for Policy-Makers*. UNESCO. Available at: https://unesdoc.unesco.org/ark:/48223/pf0000376709 (Accessed 26 January 2024).

UNESCO (2021b) *Recommendation on the Ethics of Artificial Intelligence*. UNESCO. Available at: https://unesdoc.unesco.org/ark:/48223/pf0000381137 (Accessed 26 January 2024).

6 'Understood the assignment'

A UX-led investigation into student experiences of GenAI

Kirsty Hemsworth, Alex Walker, and Jayne Evans

Introduction

The arrival of GenAI in higher education institutions (HEIs) and university classrooms will necessitate unprecedented change for academic staff and students alike. From pedagogical taxonomies and assessment practices to referencing and academic integrity, many touchstones of higher education are being interrogated in light of AI capabilities. Many academics and researchers have been early adopters of GenAI, testing the limits of large language models (LLMs) to generate plausible and publishable academic material (Altmäe et al., 2023; Macdonald et al., 2023), yet we are largely unaware of how students might be testing the limits of these platforms. While there are genuine concerns about GenAI outputs impacting authorship and intellectual property, more intriguing – at least for this chapter's authors – are how student–AI interactions shape writing processes and academic literacies. We explore how students intuitively engage with GenAI chatbots and consider how capturing this process can offer valuable insight into how undergraduate students conceptualise academic writing and GenAI literacy.

Background

Plagiarism and academic misconduct dominated early discussions of student interactions with LLMs (Barnett, 2023; Dien, 2023). Universities were swift to publish guidance on how HEIs could uphold 'academic rigour and integrity' (Russell Group, 2023). Concurrently, library and information professionals grappled with issues of acknowledgement and copyright and researchers questioned whether LLMs could be credited in publications as contributing authors (McAdoo, 2023).

Another complex issue is student behaviour surrounding GenAI – their motivations for using it, their understanding of its capabilities, and their perceptions of its ethical applications. Knee-jerk responses to LLMs have assumed that students engage with these tools to 'cut corners' (Graham, 2023) – a

DOI: 10.4324/9781003482918-8

view that risks limiting discussions of student GenAI use as remedial behaviour, similar to the framing of contract cheating as a marker of 'low academic competence' (Sweeney, 2023). Detection has been proposed as a miracle solution to these perceived threats to academic integrity, but persistent student behaviours regarding contract cheating, along with the recent discontinuation of much-publicised GenAI detection software (Nelson, 2023), suggest that productive interventions regarding GenAI use are best placed earlier in the writing process.

Approaching LLMs as tools that can help students navigate higher education offers a more positive view of GenAI and reframes the effective implementation of GenAI platforms as an alternative academic literacy and employability skill (Ewen, 2023). Practical pedagogical frameworks for GenAI use have already been developed in the field of information literacy, where database searching strategies have clear similarities to the process of prompt generation (Lo, 2023a). Just as effective literature searching involves the selection of explicit search terms – and the systematic introduction of alternate keywords and inclusion/exclusion criteria – prompt engineering for LLMs benefits from iterative refinement and the

> continuous process of testing prompts, analysing the generated AI responses, and making necessary adjustments based on observed patterns and outcomes/
>
> (Lo, 2023b)

Previously framed as an information literacy skill, students clearly need to understand the process of prompt generation and refinement to obtain relevant and reliable information from LLMs.

Prompt generation: A new academic skill?

Equally important, if students are to create explicit prompts that link to assessment criteria, is the use of instructive language over open questions. Decoding the language of assessment criteria is a core academic skill taught by learning developers, and students are encouraged to interrogate the task set by their markers and adapt their criticality as appropriate. Here, we begin to see the crossover between academic skills, information literacy, and GenAI competencies. Effective prompt generation belongs to a wider set of critical thinking and evaluation skills that enable students to extract information from assessment criteria, to identify useful research materials, and to integrate these into their academic work.

Experimentation with prompt generation for academic writing, largely focused on formulaic writing structures within scientific disciplines, has been successful (e.g. using GenAI tools to generate largely descriptive sections of scientific articles, such as abstracts, introductions, and conclusions; Altmäe et al., 2023; Macdonald et al., 2023). Particular success has been found in terms of formality, word usage, and sentence structure (Májovský et al., 2023). When testing LLMs' ability to generate scientific case studies, Buholayka et al. (2023) found that, while the omission of technical information for a professional audience was a key barrier to generating publication-compliant writing, the structure of the LLM-authored case study was largely accurate. While these studies illustrate the potential for LLMs to create well-structured pieces of academic writing, we note that the prompt iteration and refinement were undertaken in these cases by the authors. Therefore, we must interrogate the identities and experience levels of the 'academic writers' described in much existing research on GenAI (Giray, 2023): do/can undergraduate students possess the ability and contextual knowledge to translate assignment tasks into meaningful AI-appropriate prompts?

Approaching student behaviour as user experience

Screencast – where students record their interactions with digital platforms and capture all on-screen actions –is an established user experience (UX) methodology in library settings, providing insight into users' information retrieval behaviours (Conrad and Stevens, 2019), use of online library databases (Jones and Wisniewski, 2021), and website navigation (Denton et al., 2016). They offer a window on how students interact with online platforms and, if recorded in one take, can offer a largely authentic view of student behaviour. Combining screencasts with think-aloud protocols (Mathison, 2005) is particularly useful, offering additional insight into student decision-making in real time, particularly where participants are working remotely without supervision.

Several studies have applied think-aloud protocols to explore student writing, introducing an additional, reflective layer of qualitative data where written content alone is insufficient to capture the writing process. Research has considered how think-aloud protocols of assignment feedback might foster open dialogue between academic staff and students (Cunningham, 2019; Jones et al., 2012), while narrated recordings of written translation exercises offer insight into how EAL students navigate the intersections of source and target languages when self-translating (Seror, 2013). In all cases, adding think-aloud protocols aims to reduce researcher inference, offering insight into how students engage with digital technologies and writing processes, as expressed in their own words.

Method

Using an adapted UX model for usability testing (Blakiston, 2014), two Level 4 students were asked to record their screens and narrate their use of

ChatGPT-3.5 in response to a simulated assignment brief and marking criteria. Neither of the participants had any prior experience using ChatGPT-3.5: this platform was chosen as it was free to access for the participants and the functionality is largely representative of other LLMs. Both participants had heard of the tool and had expressed interest in exploring the software. This provided added value for participants – using the project as a 'dry run' to test the LLM capabilities. The participants were also beginners in essay-based writing. As Finance, Accounting, and Business students, they had experienced a range of assessment formats including report-writing, presentations, and short-answer form exams. Neither had written an extended essay-based assignment and therefore approached the task with limited knowledge of the assignment writing process.

A simulated assignment brief (Figure 6.1) was devised to allay any concerns regarding the use of GenAI chatbots with live assessments. The module title and assessment topic were invented for the purposes of the screen capture activity, following a standardised layout for assignment briefs. The activity was unscripted – participants were asked to begin their screen recording from the input of their first prompt and use the microphone to record an audio explanation of their decision-making while navigating the tool and creating an essay plan. The screen recordings were then analysed and compared by a postgraduate student, focusing on how the participants extracted information from the brief to generate prompts, and how these were refined based on the text outputs in ChatGPT-3.5. This was enhanced by a written reflection submitted by both participants once the analysis was completed to address any gaps in the recordings where researcher inference risked skewing the results.

Screencast analysis

From their opening prompts, we noted that, despite their lack of experience using LLMs, both participants approached the task with preconceptions about the tool's capabilities. Both opened with questions, seeking information on how to approach the *task* of writing an extended essay, rather than generating any content. Participant A seemed to conceptualise ChatGPT-3.5 as a search engine rather than a generative tool. They judged the quality of the content based on its replicability:

> I found that each time I asked a question, it showed slightly different answers. So I was hoping for some consistency . . . unfortunately [there] wasn't a lot. There was a question I asked regarding good recommendations in financial literacy in universities. [The answer] was not what I was hoping for, so I tried a different way of searching.

Assessment Task

Module title	Finance in Context
Assessment topic	Financial Literacy Education in Universities
Assessment type	Essay
Word count	2000 +/- 10%
Weighting	50%
Submission date	Friday 3 November 2023

Assessment brief

You are required to write and submit a 2000-word essay exploring the topic of financial literacy education in universities, examining the importance and impact of financial literacy training for students experiencing the challenges of the cost-of-living crisis and the effects of the Covid-19 pandemic.

LO1: To identify the importance of financial literacy in Higher Education.

Students will critically assess the significance of financial literacy education in higher education, examining its impact on students' financial well-being and financial success. They will identify key reasons why financial literacy education is an important for universities to provide as part of their student support offers.

LO2: To examine current financial literacy initiatives in UK universities, identifying strengths and challenges.

Students will investigate and compare existing financial literacy initiatives in universities. They will evaluate different approaches, programs, or resources aimed at enhancing students' money management skills, and assess their effectiveness and common challenges.

LO3: Propose practical recommendations or guidelines for universities to enhance their financial literacy support.

Students will synthesise their understanding of the importance of financial literacy and insights from existing initiatives to suggest practical recommendations for universities to enhance financial literacy education.

Figure 6.1 The assessment brief used by participants.

The term 'searching' here is particularly revealing – Participant A followed a literature-searching process, demonstrating some awareness of the importance of quality academic sources in their prompt construction. Their subsequent prompts repeated this evaluative language: '*what are good recommendations for "financial literacy education in universities" essays?*' The use of speech marks in these prompts also suggests prior knowledge of phrase searching – a skill commonly used in library database searching – which again alludes to their conceptualisation of the LLM as an information discovery tool.

Later, Participant A narrowed their search by directly quoting keywords from the assessment brief to enhance their prompts. However, the results of this search were deemed unsatisfactory – the prompt was misinterpreted and the LLM generated suggested essay subheadings and content. The student reacted over the microphone, redirecting the LLM to act as search engine, rather than text generator:

> this was not what I was looking for – I was looking for some book recommendations or articles . . . I'm going to do that again.

However, through this process, Participant A demonstrated basic 'iterative refinement' skills (Lo, 2023) – they followed up with a clear statement to redirect the LLM: '*book recommendation for financial literacy education in universities*'.

However, by overlooking ChatGPT-3.5's generative capabilities and viewing the text outputs as information retrieval results, Participant A failed to identify when the tool produced fabricated content. Several book recommendations were hallucinations (Li et al., 2023; Májovský et al., 2023). Participant A missed this, despite spelling mistakes in some of the generated content, and continued to be preoccupied with the specificity and refinement of their inputs using literature-searching strategies – they introduced 'higher education' and 'UK' as additional search terms – rather than considering that the quality of the outputs may be compromised.

Participant B demonstrated a stronger understanding of ChatGPT-3.5's generative capabilities and described engaging with the tool in conversation:

> 'I was hoping to start a natural conversation like you would with a peer if you didn't know something' (using text outputs to supplement existing subject knowledge)
> 'I used ChatGPT-3.5 as a guide like talking to a fellow peer on tips or advice'.

Starting from an opening question regarding essay structure, Participant B adopted a broad-to-narrow approach, narrating how they intended to redirect their prompts towards generating useable content: '*what subheadings should i use to write an academic essay on financial literacy*'. Here, they alluded to their knowledge of subheadings as a useful tool for organising academic content but did not refer to the assessment brief, which provided a three-part structure for students to follow. Instead, we see that Student B's essay plan (Figure 6.2) closely mirrors the presentation of information in the chat window, suggesting that the organisation of AI-generated responses has a direct impact on how students structure their academic work:

Participant B's prompt refinement followed a top-down approach: from each response, they selected a keyword and requested more detail. Where the relationship between the generated subheadings was unclear, Participant B sought clarification – '*how does financial literacy relate to income, expenses and budgeting?*' – in an effort to filter out irrelevant information from the long list of content generated by a previous prompt. The result was a detailed essay plan, laid out in a clear bullet-pointed structure that stretched beyond the scope of the initial prompt. However, at no point in the recording did the student return to the brief to check the relevance of the AI-generated content, or whether the volume of content they had amassed would fit the assessment word count. Here, we see an inquisitive but ultimately distracted exploration of topics such as Chilean pension reform and credit counselling in Singapore, facilitated by the LLM.

Both participants recognised that their ability to effectively use ChatGPT-3.5 could be improved with further practice, suggesting that

---

1. **Introduction:**
    - Definition and importance of financial literacy
        - Management of money and personal finance
        - Making informed financial decisions
        - Interpret financial information
    - Brief overview of the essay's structure

2. **The Basics of Financial Literacy**
    - Understanding financial literacy
    - Key concepts: income, expenses, budgeting

3. **Case Studies and Success Stories**

    - Examples of individuals benefiting from financial literacy
        - Credit counselling in Singapore case study (2004)
        - Chilean pension reform
        - Mexican financial education for micro-entrepreneurs

Figure 6.2 Transcription of Student B's essay plan, showing subheading and bullet-point structure copied directly from GenAI.

GenAI use is approached as a skill to be developed. Participant A felt that the key to improving their use of the tool was in refining their questions to produce accurate and replicable information, while Participant B expressed an interest in testing out more complex tasks, such as *'giving ChatGPT-3.5 some background information and then asking it a question about the information'*. These reflections on future use align with the approach of each student: Participant A views the LLM as a search engine and a means of discovering accurate information, while Participant B has a stronger awareness of its generative abilities and applications. After using ChatGPT-3.5 for the first time, both participants reflected on its value and relevance for academic writing, yet their preconceptions about *how* to use the tool remained fixed.

Recommendations for practice

These recorded interactions offer only the slightest of glimpses into how students might engage with GenAI platforms to inform, craft, and refine their academic writing. Yet, the implications are clear: academic writing, and the set of analytical and evaluative skills that this encompasses, is a process that cannot remain untouched by the transformative effects of GenAI. GenAI has inverted the taxonomy upon which so many of our pedagogical approaches are based: the creation of new knowledge is no longer the preserve of the experts, but a skill opened to all learners with a single prompt (Rivers and Holland, 2023). Yet, as our screen recordings revealed, beginner users can quickly move into self-directed conversations with LLMs, with each stage of the exchange determined by the perceived relevance of the generated content, rather than a pre-planned set of prompts or structured set of assessment criteria.

As a result of this study, we propose four key recommendations for developing AI-literacy which we are now integrating into a university-wide academic skills programme, supported by a team of student partners:

1. **Start with prompts**
   Prompt generation is a powerful tool that combines information literacy skills and the instructive language of written assessments. We will include demonstration of how to craft specific and analytical prompts in our core academic writing sessions, using examples of assignment briefs and genuine AI responses to scaffold teaching.

2. **Foster GenAI literacy as a skillset**
   Approaching GenAI literacy as a competence-based skillset opens up the possibility for all learners to approach GenAI use as a developmental process. We will develop new content on GenAI applications that connect academic and employability skills, using relevant frameworks to encourage students to track their digital competencies.

3. **Encourage critical evaluation**

   Students require skills and confidence to assess the relevance of LLM outputs and to decide about their application within their specific academic disciplines. We will update the examples in our academic skills sessions to engage students in up-to-date conversations around ethical applications of GenAI.

4. **Embrace UX methodologies**

   Understanding how students interact with GenAI tools is crucial to develop responsive approaches to teaching AI literacy. We will expand the UX methodology used in this study to build a database of student interactions with GenAI to inform teaching, learning, and assessment approaches.

Although brief, our recordings offer a glimpse of GenAI–student interactions. They suggest that UX methodologies have the potential to capture specific moments in which GenAI tools influence and inform student approaches to academic writing. Perhaps most exciting is the possibility that this approach can offer insight into how less visible students – those hesitant to seek support or engage in 'remedial' development activities – might capitalise on the anonymity of interactions with GenAI tools to experiment with, and develop, their academic writing skills.

Critical appraisal

Zayne Knight, MSc Cancer Biology

On my course, we have been informed of the unreliable nature of some GenAI tools and issues of plagiarism, but not discouraged from using them. GenAI has the potential to be an excellent tool and is already useful for mathematics and identifying data trends in my field. I feel that the same methodology which this chapter has used would be a reliable way to test the capabilities of GenAI tools for programming and more advanced data analysis.

I have used GenAI tools to offer more information on selected topics, particularly for definitions and explanations. An example of a prompt I would use is: 'What are nanoparticles and explain how they are able to treat cancer' and I would ask a follow-up question such as, 'Could you provide academic references to support this information?' As I have experienced, the GenAI tool will provide references, however, many of these references do not work or have been redacted from papers.

When reflecting on the study chapter, I realised that the prompts used by beginners are quite general and could be broken down into more specific searches.

References

Altmäe, S., Sola-Leyva, A. and Salumets, A. (2023) Artificial intelligence in scientific writing: A friend or a foe? *Reproductive BioMedicine Online*, 47(1), pp. 3–9. Available at: https://doi.org/10.1016/j.rbmo.2023.04.009 (Accessed 26 January 2024).

Barnett, S. (2023) ChatGPT-3.5 is making universities rethink plagiarism. *Wired*, 30 January. Available at: www.wired.com/story/ChatGPT-3.5-college-university-plagiarism/ (Accessed 20 September 2023).

Blakiston, L. (2014) *Usability Testing: A Practical Guide for Librarians.* Maryland: Rowman & Littlefield.

Buholayka, M., Zouabi, R. and Tadinada, A. (2023) The readiness of ChatGPT-3.5 to write scientific case reports independently: A comparative evaluation between human and artificial intelligence. *Cureus*, 15(5). Available at: https://doi.org/10.7759/cureus.39386 (Accessed 26 January 2024).

Conrad, S. and Stevens, C. (2019) 'Am I on the library website?': A Lib-Guides usability study. *Information Technology and Libraries*, 38(3), pp. 49–81. Available at: https://doi.org/10.6017/ital.v38i3.10977 (Accessed 26 January 2024).

Cunningham, K. (2019) Student perceptions and use of technology-mediated text and screencast feedback in ESL writing. *Computers and Composition*, 52, pp. 222–241. Available at: https://doi.org/10.1016/j.compcom.2019.02.003 (Accessed 26 January 2024).

Denton, A., Moody, D. and Bennett, J. (2016) Usability testing as a method to refine a health sciences library website. *Medical Reference Services Quarterly*, 35(1), pp. 1–15. Available at: https://doi.org/10.1080/02763869.2016.1117280 (Accessed 26 January 2024).

Dien, J. (2023) Editorial: Generative artificial intelligence as a plagiarism problem. *Biological Psychology*, 181. Available at: https://doi.org/10.1016/j.biopsycho.2023.108621 (Accessed 26 January 2024).

Ewen, M. (2023) Mapping the potential of AI in the age of competence based higher education. *WonkHE*, 20 February. Available at: https://wonkhe.com/blogs/mapping-the-potential-of-ai-in-the-age-of-competence-based-higher-education (Accessed 10 September 2023).

Giray, L. (2023) Prompt engineering with ChatGPT-3.5: A guide for academic writers. *Annals of Biomedical Engineering*. Available at: https://doi.org/10.1007/s10439-023-03272-4 (Accessed 26 January 2024).

Graham, A. (2023) ChatGPT-3.5 and other AI tools put students at risk of plagiarism allegations, MDU warns. *BMJ*, 381, p. 1133. Available at: https://doi.org/10.1136/bmj.p1133 (Accessed 26 January 2024).

Jones, E. and Wisniewski, C. (2021) Video killed the multiple-choice quiz: Capturing students' literature searching skills using a screencast video assignment. *Journal of the Medical Library Association*, 109(4). Available at: https://doi.org/10.5195/jmla.2021.1270 (Accessed 26 January 2024).

Jones, N., Georghiades, P. and Gunson, J. (2012) Student feedback via screen capture digital video: Stimulating student's modified action. *Higher Education*, 64, pp. 593–607. Available at: https://doi.org/10.1007/s10734-012-9514-7 (Accessed 26 January 2024).

Li, Y et al. (2023) Can large language models write reflectively? *Computers and Education: Artificial Intelligence*, 4. Available at: https://doi.org/10.1016/j.caeai.2023.100140 (Accessed 26 January 2024).

Lo, L.S. (2023a) The art and science of prompt engineering: A new literacy in the information age. *Internet Reference Services Quarterly*, pp. 1–8. Available at: https://doi.org/10.1080/10875301.2023.2227621 (Accessed 26 January 2024).

Lo, L.S. (2023b) The CLEAR path: A framework for enhancing information literacy through prompt engineering. *The Journal of Academic Librarianship*, 49(4). Available at: https://doi.org/10.1016/j.acalib.2023.102720 (Accessed 26 January 2024).

Macdonald, C. et al. (2023) Can ChatGPT-3.5 draft a research article? An example of population-level vaccine effectiveness analysis. *Journal of Global Health*, 13. Available at: https://doi.org/10.7189/JOGH.13.01003 (Accessed 26 January 2024).

Májovský, M. et al. (2023) Artificial intelligence can generate fraudulent but authentic-looking scientific medical articles: Pandora's box has been opened. *Journal of Medical Internet Research*, 25. Available at: https://doi.org/10.2196/46924 (Accessed 26 January 2024).

Mathison, S. (Ed.) (2005) *Encyclopedia of Evaluation*. New York: SAGE.

McAdoo, T. (2023) *How to cite ChatGPT-3.5*. American Psychological Association, 7 April. Available at: https://apastyle.apa.org/blog/how-to-cite-ChatGPT-3.5 (Accessed 20 September 2023).

Nelson, J. (2023) OpenAI quietly shuts down its AI detection tool. *Decrypt*, 24 July. Available at: https://decrypt.co/149826/openai-quietly-shutters-its-ai-detection-tool (Accessed 11 September 2023).

Rivers, C. and Holland, A. (2023) How can generative AI intersect with Bloom's taxonomy? *Times Higher Education*, 30 August. Available at: www.timeshighereducation.com/campus/how-can-generative-ai-intersect-blooms-taxonomy (Accessed 19 September 2023).

Russell Group (2023) New principles on use of AI in education. *Russel Group*, 4 July. Available at: https://russellgroup.ac.uk/news/new-principles-on-use-of-ai-in-education/ (Accessed 8 September 2023).

Seror, J. (2013) Screen capture technology: A digital window into students' writing processes/Technologie de capture d'écran: une fenêtre numérique sur le processus d'écriture des étudiants. *Canadian Journal of Learning and Technology/La revue canadienne de l'apprentissage et de la technologie*, 39(3). Available at: https://doi.org/10.21432/T28G6K (Accessed 26 January 2024).

Sweeney, S. (2023) Who wrote this? Essay mills and assessment – considerations regarding contract cheating and AI in higher education. *The International Journal of Management Education*, 21(2). Available at: https://doi.org/10.1016/j.ijme.2023.100818 (Accessed 26 January 2024).

Part C

Curriculum design for a generative AI-enabled world

7 Re-imagining student engagement in an AI-enhanced classroom

Strategies and practices

Hazel Farrell

Introduction

The rapid evolution of generative artificial intelligence (GenAI) has stimulated a frenzy of activity in the field of education as ethical considerations are debated and regulation is sought to reign in one of the fastest-growing technologies of the digital age. However, a gradual shift towards a more positive acknowledgement of the practical benefits for learners and educators has become evident, albeit with a prevailing cautious undertone (Escotet, 2023), (Sharples, 2023). Emerging research attempts to capture the intricacies of the narrative while also suggesting potential approaches to move forward in the wake of the GenAI disruption (Sabzalieva and Valentini 2023), (Nerantzi et al., 2023). While Arnold (2023) identifies the three main responses as revert, outrun, and embrace, it has since become clear that the latter is the only viable option, and the necessity for educators to evolve to ensure the relevance of their pedagogies in preparing learners for an AI-enabled society cannot be denied. Mollick (2023) discusses the transformative role of GenAI with reference to the 'flipped concept' where GenAI serves as a personal tutor for knowledge acquisition and the building of foundational skills in the home, thereby providing scope for deeper learning experiences in the classroom. The significant level of learner investment integral to this model necessitates effective student engagement practices to optimise the benefits.

Context

The opportunities presented by GenAI aligned directly with ongoing explorations to enhance student engagement and create meaningful learning experiences. The early adoption of this disruptive technology was strategic in confronting challenges around academic integrity through transparency, student-led discussion, and peer learning. The study encompasses a small sample of 18 students from years 1, 3, and 4 of the music degree programme in South East Technological University undertaking research, history, and

DOI: 10.4324/9781003482918-10

dissertation modules. ChatGPT-3.5 and, subsequently, ChatGPT-4 were chosen based on their prominence in the narrative around GenAI and education.

Methods

Inspired by the ethos of Mollick's 'flipped concept', an AI-enhanced exploration of activities focusing on higher-order skills such as evaluation and creation supported by ideation, structuring, and feedback, was adopted. A collaborative approach was integral in stimulating active learning, particularly for more complex tasks (Boud, 2000). Transparency and engagement with the process were ensured through an AI declaration form developed to accompany module assessments, requiring information on which tool was used, what it was used for, and the impact of GenAI on the submission. Further data was collected in an end-of-semester student survey reflecting on the GenAI learning experience.

Application

The activities detailed below took place in the classroom and concentrate predominantly on 'assessment as learning' (Liu and Bridgeman, 2023) thereby highlighting the significance of the process rather than a final artefact (Lodge, 2023).

Evaluating GenAI

Following the completion of a low-stakes assessment to research and write a programme note on a piece of music being performed by each student, ChatGPT-3.5 was prompted to undertake the same exercise. Drawing on their foundational knowledge, the group evaluated the GenAI results.

Ideation and initiation of a sustainability in the arts festival

A Socratic approach was adopted as ChatGPT-3.5 was prompted to provide suggestions on how sustainability applies to music, leading to more specific prompts on events, initiatives, and musicians associated with the concept. Each learner selected an element that resonated with them as a focus for their research and contribution to the festival.

Structuring

GenAI was used both inside and outside the classroom to suggest structures for assessments including presentations and research assignments.

Choosing dissertation topics

ChatGPT 4 was prompted to suggest viable research topics around broad areas of interest proposed by students, resulting in a list of 10 potential topics for each. Following a further prompt, it generated a reading list of 15 items for selected topics including journal articles, book chapters, and interviews, supplemented with information on the relevance of each source to the topic.

Alternative titles

ChatGPT 4 was prompted to suggest alternative titles for a wide variety of works including presentations, dissertations, and chapters, serving to highlight whether the original title accurately reflected the content and provide options for creative refinement.

Marking rubrics

A dissertation marking rubric was created collaboratively, following which an AI rubric was generated. A comparative analysis was undertaken resulting in a modified marking rubric.

Feedback

Dissertation students copied specific sections of their work into ChatGPT 4 and asked for feedback regarding clarity. Comments and recommendations on clarity ensued including a summary of their material, thereby enabling students to determine if their work needed further development before submission.

While this study applies to a music degree programme, the transferability to other disciplines and education settings is clearly evident given the focus on research-based module types.

Discussion and findings

These activities exemplify the potential for GenAI not only to be 'a natural ally' for authentic assessments (Arnold, 2023) but also to facilitate deeper learning experiences. The necessity for active engagement served to increase learner investment in the module content and assessment processes. This was enhanced by the collaborative approach which Escotet (2023) suggests can improve educational and psychological outcomes.

Educator's observations

Activities involving critical evaluation of GenAI outputs had a notable impact, including group recognition that prior knowledge of the subject matter was necessary to identify omissions or contextual implications. This was particularly valuable in managing future aspirations for the use of GenAI for academic work. Further observations included dissatisfaction with the enthusing rather than subjective tone, leading to enquiries around bias. A profound learning moment occurred when gender, race, and culture were presented by GenAI as potential biases.

The emergence of repetitive patterns and stock phrases also raised concerns in repeated iterations of the same exercise, for instance, Arvo Pärt's *Spiegel im Spiegel* is described by GenAI as 'a true gem of minimalist music' and Scarlatti's *Piano Sonata in A major* as 'a true gem of baroque music'. Discipline-specific considerations were also raised in relation to the distribution of marks in the GenAI rubric resulting in a higher weighting being suggested by the group for analytical content. The identification of 'flaws' with the GenAI output served to remind the group of the value of their own work, thereby placing empowerment of the student voice at the core of this learning experience.

The use of GenAI for ideation, structuring, and reviewing assignments in a group setting introduced learners to possibilities for consolidating core foundational skills, thereby encouraging experimentation beyond the classroom to suit their own learning needs. Guidance on moving past the blank page and creating well-structured documents supported by personalised and timely feedback naturally fosters confidence, enhances productivity, and has the potential to improve quality.

Integrity and fairness emerged as concerns for students in group discussions and therefore a mechanism to declare GenAI usage was welcomed. The small sample was recognised as a positive in mitigating against challenges associated with anonymity in large class sizes. Despite this, one incident of cheating did emerge involving a combination of GenAI and an AI paraphrasing tool, with absenteeism and lack of engagement as underlying factors. The identification of accessibility to contract cheating services as a major factor in academic misconduct (Lines, 2016) may also be applied here as GenAI tools increasingly permeate our educational and social platforms.

Student feedback

Results of the declaration form revealed ChatGPT-3.5 (39%) and -4 (39%) as the main tools chosen independently by students to use beyond the classroom, with Grammarly and Quillbot (22%) to a lesser extent. Evaluations of the impact of GenAI on submitted assignments tended to stray into descriptions of usage; however, a higher quality of work was suggested with references to improved structure, focus, efficiency, and engagement.

Survey results identified GenAI usage for structuring as the most popular, followed by ideation and research, see Figure 1.1. Personalised learning in

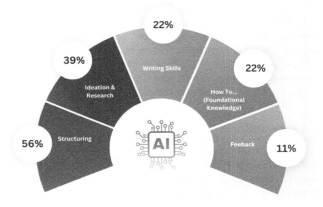

Figure 7.1 Survey results on student usage of GenAI (18 participants, multiple answers permitted).

relation to improving weaknesses and knowledge acquisition emerged equally, while feedback was highlighted by a smaller number of learners in association with dissertation, reflecting the more advanced stage of their learning journey.

While the majority of participants (61%) felt that GenAI enhanced their learning experience, a notable number remained undecided (28%). Those who answered 'No' (11%) opted for limited engagement with GenAI in the completion of their assignments, perhaps suggesting a reluctance to change. Concerns included references to responsible use and the over-reliance on GenAI not equating to 'real learning'; however, enthusiasm for a continued exploration of GenAI also emerged.

Conclusions

The introduction of GenAI in a transparent and collaborative manner was integral in stimulating active engagement among learners while also reminding them of the value of their own voices. This positioned them to engage with GenAI independently beyond the classroom. The question of equity requires consideration in relation to the choice, and ability, of some learners to pay for more advanced versions.

Clear guidance around GenAI usage was sought by learners, highlighting their investment in establishing a culture of integrity and the need to carefully consider appropriate discipline or module-specific applications. In addition to continuing assessment redesign with focus on the process to present opportunities for deeper learning experiences, guidelines on GenAI usage will accompany all future assignment briefs. The independent use of AI paraphrasing tools also presents a challenge, requiring discussion and regulation.

Further clarification on the evaluation aspect of the declaration form emerged as requiring reinforcement to capture impact rather than descriptions of GenAI usage. Despite these challenges, the early adoption of this continuously evolving technology was largely successful and the implicit learning has been invaluable in informing future practice.

Critical appraisal

Aaron O'Rourke, final year music student, South East Technology University This study explores the many ways that GenAI can be integrated as a tool to aid students in their academic studies, exploring both the benefits and limitations as well as how it can enhance the learning experience. As a student I was a part of this study, primarily using ChatGPT to help generate suggestions for viable research topics for my dissertation. It was also used in my analysis and history modules to evaluate the GenAI outputs on different styles of music. I was amazed by the ability of GenAI to take a broad topic such as minimalism and break it down in such a detailed and succinct manner, while acknowledging that the information was not absolute. In the case of my dissertation topic and reading list, a wide variety of viable angles and research materials were suggested that I may have overlooked otherwise. As a result, I have used GenAI to help gather resources for my studies, specifically aiding in data collection and in tasks such as structuring. Through my use of GenAI, I recognise the importance of being the author of my own work and while GenAI may be useful in many practical applications, it is no substitute for human creativity and originality.

References

Arnold, L. (2023) AI and assessment in higher education: Reflections. *Blogpost*, 13 February. Available at: https://lydia-arnold.com/2023/02/15/ai-and-assessment-in-higher-education-reflections/ (Accessed 30 July 2023).

Boud, D. (2000) Sustainable assessment: Rethinking assessment for the learning society. *Studies in Continuing Education*, 22(2), pp. 151–167. Available at: https://doi.org/10.1080/713695728.

Escotet, M.Á. (2023) *The Optimistic Future of Artificial Intelligence in Higher Education*. Prospects UNESCO BIE. Available at: https://doi.org/10.1007/s11125-023-09642-z (Accessed 1 September 2023).

Lines, L. (2016) Ghostwriters guaranteeing grades? The quality of online ghostwriting services available to tertiary students in Australia. *Teaching in*

Higher Education, 21(8), pp. 889–914. Available at: https://doi.org/10.108 0/13562517.2016.1198759.

Liu, D. and Bridgeman, A. (2023) *What to Do about Assessments If We Can't Out-Design or Out-Run AI?* Available at: https://educational-innovation. sydney.edu.au/teaching@sydney/what-to-do-about-assessments-if-we-cant-out-design-or-out-run-ai/ (Accessed 1 September 2023).

Lodge, J.M. (2023) *Assessing Learning Processes Instead of Artefacts Won't be Easy*. Available at: www.linkedin.com/pulse/assessing-learning-processes-instead-artefacts-wont-easy-lodge/ (Accessed 1 September 2023).

Mollick, E. (2023) The future of education in a world of AI: A positive vision for the transformation to come. *Blogpost*, 9 April. Available at: www.oneuse-fulthing.org/p/the-future-of-education-in-a-world (Accessed 30 July 2023).

Nerantzi, C., Abegglen, S., Karatsiori, M. and Martinez-Arboleda, A. (Eds.) (2023) *101 Creative Ideas to Use AI in Education. A Collection Curated by #creativeHE*. CC-BY-NC-SA 4.0. Available at: https://zenodo.org/record/8072950.

Sabzalieva, E. and Valentini, A. (2023) *ChatGPT and Artificial Intelligence in Higher Education: Quick Start Guide*. UNESCO. Available at: www.iesalc. unesco.org/wp-content/uploads/2023/04/ChatGPT-and-Artificial-Intelligence-in-higher-education-Quick-Start-guide_EN_FINAL.pdf (Accessed 1 September 2023).

Sharples, M. (2023) *Generative AI: Transforming Higher Education. Webinar Sharing Learning*. Open University of Catalonia, 7 June. Available at: www.youtube.com/watch?v=v8A0xix0Ofo.

8 The potential of AI text-to-image generation in medical education

The educator and students' perspective

Pierce Burr, Ajay Kumar, and Tim Young

Introduction

Medical education traditionally depends on patient images to educate doctors in training to recognise medical conditions visually. There are some critical challenges with this traditional approach. For rare medical conditions, the educator may not have access to a suitable photograph. Additionally, concerns regarding patient consent and confidentiality present significant barriers to accessing and storing medical images (Hill, 2006).

The recent introduction of high-quality text-to-image generative AI (GenAI) tools allows an alternative approach to create such images. The ability to mentally picture visual representations based on description is a fundamental part of human cognition. Text-to-image GenAI likewise produces accurate visual content based on descriptive textual input. This is achieved through deep learning algorithms implemented into neural networks which are trained using large datasets of varied images paired with accurate descriptors (Frolov et al., 2021).

It is now possible to rapidly create photographic quality images using simple text prompts to produce unique medical images without compromising patient confidentiality. Theoretically, these could illustrate many medical conditions with enormous potential for medical education. Surprisingly, little has yet been published in this field, with most studies focusing more on the use of GenAI in medical diagnosis rather than education (Adams et al., 2023; Kather et al., 2022).

This proof-of-concept project involved two postgraduate students (both medical doctors) along with their course professor. The students received a small stipend funding for their participation from University College London (UCL).

Limitations of text-to-image GenAI for disease representation to date

The limited published literature to date on this nascent approach in medical education has suggested some cautious optimism in teaching plastic surgeon

DOI: 10.4324/9781003482918-11

trainees and for producing histopathology illustration, yet showing suboptimal fidelity of disease representation for skin conditions and various radiology modalities (Koljonen, 2023; Kather et al., 2022; Cheraghlou, 2023; Miftahul Amri and Khairatun Hisan, 2023; Adams et al., 2023). GenAI is however developing so rapidly that adequate medical images may soon be possible in such cases.

Generated examples of currently available text-to-image GenAI

We now demonstrate illustrative examples of work we have created with widely available GenAI text-to-image generation tools. These are *not* photos and do not show images of any individual patient.

Figure 8.1 shows a large pupil (the dark central part of the eye) despite a light being shone towards the eye. Normally, the pupils constrict in response to bright light. This may not occur with certain pathological conditions such as optic neuritis, which can occur in multiple sclerosis. This image was generated from the text prompt: a photograph of a female with a light shining in her eye but the pupil is very large.

In the next example (Figure 8.2), we consider the common general medical scenario of a neck swelling. The wide potential differential diagnosis of midline anterior neck swellings is broad, yet thyroid swellings are common and important for all doctors to be aware of. A particular challenge of conventional medical photography occurs when the patient's face must be shown as this raises issues of confidentiality. With GenAI text-to-image generation, this challenge can be overcome.

She is depicted from a front-facing view, with the neck area clearly visible. The thyroid gland should be noticeably enlarged and asymmetrical, occupying a significant portion of the neck and extending slightly beyond the usual

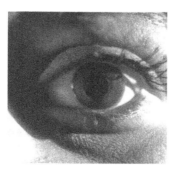

Figure 8.1 Abnormally large pupil size despite light stimulus. Generated using DALLE-2.

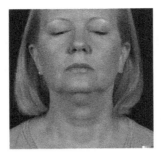

Figure 8.2 Potential thyroid gland swelling generated using DALL-E2. Text prompt (generated using ChatGPT): 'High quality image of female patient with neck swelling'.

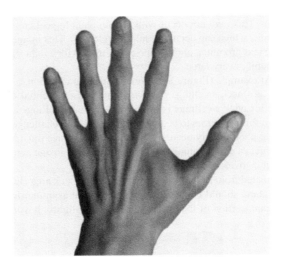

Figure 8.3 Illustration of swollen finger joints in keeping with arthritis and associated muscle wasting. Generated using DALLE-2.

boundaries. The middle of the neck should have a lobulated appearance, indicating the presence of nodules."

Other common medical conditions can likewise be represented, Figure 8.3 shows a representation of the appearance of arthritis in the hand.

In addition to photographic quality images, we also explored the potential of GenAI text-to-image tools in promoting reflective activities and developing the ideas of Huston and Kaminski (Huston and Kaminski, 2023). For

Figure 8.4 Image generated to illustrate an artistic interpretation of a medical image designed to encourage reflection beyond more typical factual elements. Generated using DALLE-2.

example, Figure 8.4 is generated from the prompt: 'A neurosurgeon operating on a brain in the style of Monet'.

Figure 8.5 shows an image of medical staff which can be used to help illustrate cases being described to students. For example, giving a student a hypothetical medical case, then showing this image and asking: 'What should the doctors consider in their deliberations?'

Review of text-to-image GenAI from the perspective of the student and educator

To date, only a limited number of published studies have considered the potential of text-to-image GenAI for medical education with some concerns of suboptimal image fidelity, for dermatological and radiological images at least (Koljonen, 2023; Adams et al., 2023). This may reflect a fundamental design limitation in most available text-to-image software currently which explicitly discourages the generation of images depicting injuries or illnesses (DALL-E2 Content Policy, 2023). While this may be understandable to help protect against potentially distressing images being posted on public forums, this is a limitation for medical educators trying to generate pathological images. Despite this, our group was able to produce workable illustrations

Figure 8.5 Illustration of doctors discussing a case. Image produced using DALLE-3 based on the text prompt: '2 doctors at work on ward wearing scrubs, 1 female, 1 male, detailed, professional, sharp focus, no blur, photorealism, HD quality, 8k resolution'.

of medical conditions using GenAI text-to-image generators currently widely available (Figures 8.1–8.3).

It is unknown currently if actual medical images were included in the training data of the currently available text-to-image GenAI software (Sarp et al., 2021). By increasing the quality and quantity of medical images in the training data, more accurate end-product images would be expected with text-to-image GenAI tools. However, the ethical considerations are as large as the potential benefits. High-fidelity medical text-to-image GenAI raises issues of consent and possibly of image access. The danger of 'deepfake' images spreading misinformation is a concerning possibility. Furthermore, medical text-to-image GenAI training relies on the data supplied, which may overrepresent or underrepresent certain ethnicities and therefore further potentiate bias (Guo et al., 2022). Finally, if actual medical images are to be used in future GenAI training, to what extent is consent needed for the use of the original images?

Reflection from the students co-authors

Both student co-authors reflected on this project and overall, views were favourable. For example, in the picture shown in Figure 8.2, one wrote: 'the neck swelling does look very realistic'. However, limitations were also noted:

'It's easier to create images of skin and other swellings than complicated symptoms (or signs) like in Horner syndrome'. The overall reflections were that the use of GenAI to produce images for medical education represented a great opportunity, while acknowledging limitations: 'Benefits should be not overstated but neither should the potential opportunities be dismissed'.

Conclusion

The integration of GenAI networks and technologies within medical practice appears inevitable. Early exposure to these technologies in medical education would allow medical students to both benefit from the learning opportunities and gain a deeper understanding of GenAI. The appetite of medical students to be exposed to, and understand, such technologies and their perception of the future role of GenAI in the future of medical practice is strong (Buabbas et al., 2023; Civaner et al., 2022).

Despite the limitations, we have shown in this chapter that it is possible to produce usable medical illustrations for medical education using currently available GenAI tools. The future seems likely to offer greater capabilities – and challenges – in the use of GenAI text-to-image generation for medical education.

Acknowledgements

The authors are very grateful to the University College London Arena Changemakers team for their support of this project. This took the form of a £600 student stipend (shared equally between the students) to help allow them the time to participate in this study.

GenAI tools used in this project:

Go Art Version 3.4.1.114: Images generated Jan–August 2023. Publisher: Everimaging Science and Technology Co., Ltd.

Chat GPT 3.5: Text generated by ChatGPT July–August, 2023. OpenAI, https://chat.openai.com. ChatGPT.

DALLE-2: images generated by DALLE-2 July–August, 2023. OpenAI, https://openai.com/dall-e-2.

Critical appraisal

Prof. Kathleen Armour, Vice Provost (Education and Student Experience), UCL

I am an educator, so I have reflected on this chapter from that perspective. In my current role, I have responsibility for education across the university, and the rise of AI (particularly Chat GPT) has prompted a flurry of new anxieties and responses from staff and students. At UCL, we established a multi-disciplinary AI 'expert' group to help us think through the challenges and opportunities posed by AI, although we quickly acknowledged that none of us is an expert on the medium-/long-term implications of AI for society. This means that the future remains to be shaped, which is both daunting and exciting. We also funded students to work with staff to investigate some of the implications of AI for learning in their discipline, and that is the genesis of the study reported in this paper.

The paper illustrates several of the issues with which we are grappling currently. For example, at the outset, the authors note that studies have tended to focus on the diagnostic potential of AI, rather than the educational potential, and this is a common problem. Yet, despite the immediate fears around assessment integrity, it is in education that some of the real benefits of AI can be realised. The authors also point to the ethics issues that are arising and to which there are few or inadequate answers at this stage. Nonetheless, as they conclude: 'text-to-image AI is here to stay', so the interesting questions raised by this work are: how can we develop optimal models of human–AI interaction in medical education; and how are we ensuring that AI developers are designing what we want and need? This paper makes an interesting contribution to the debates around these questions.

References

Adams, L.C., Busch, F., Truhn, D., Makowski, M.R., Aerts, H.J.W.L. and Bressem, K. (2023) What does DALL-E 2 know about radiology? *Journal of Medical Internet Research*, 23. Available at: https://doi.org/10.2196/43110.

Buabbas, A.J., Miskin, B., Alnaqi, A.A., Ayed, A.K., Shehab, A.A., Syed-Abdul, S. and Uddin, M. (2023) Investigating students' perceptions towards artificial intelligence in medical education. *Healthcare*, 11(9), p. 1298. Available at: https://doi.org/10.3390/healthcare11091298.

Cheraghlou, S. (2023) Evaluating dermatologic domain knowledge in DALL-E 2 and potential applications for dermatology-specific algorithms. *International Journal of Dermatology*, 62(10), pp. e521–e523. Available at: https://doi.org/10.1111/IJD.16683.

Civaner, M.M., Uncu, Y., Bulut, F., Chalil, E.G. and Tali, A. (2022) Artificial intelligence in medical education: A cross-sectional needs assessment. *BMC Medical Education*, 22(1). Available at: https://doi.org/10.1186/S12909-022-03852-3.

DALL-E2 Content Policy (2023) *Are there Any Restrictions to How I Can Use DALL·E 2? Is there a Content Policy?* OpenAI Help Center. Available at: https://help.openai.com/en/articles/6338764-are-there-any-restrictions-to-how-i-can-use-dall-e-2-is-there-a-content-policy (Accessed 7 July 2023).

Frolov, S., Hinz, T., Roue, F., Hees, J. and Dengel, A. (2021) Adversarial text-to-image synthesis: A review. *Neural Networks*, 144, pp. 187–209. Available at: https://doi.org/10.1016/J.NEUNET.2021.07.019.

Guo, L.N., Lee, M.S., Kassamali, B., Mita, C. and Nambudiri, V.E. (2022) Bias in, bias out: Underreporting and underrepresentation of diverse skin types in machine learning research for skin cancer detection-A scoping review. *Journal of the American Academy of Dermatology*, 87(1), pp. 157–159. Available at: https://doi.org/10.1016/J.JAAD.2021.06.884.

Hill, K. (2006) Consent, confidentiality and record keeping for the recording and usage of medical images. *Journal of Visual Communication in Medicine*, 28(2), pp. 76–79. Available at: https://doi.org/10.1080/01405110600863365.

Huston, J.C. and Kaminski, N. (2023) A picture worth a thousand words, created with one sentence: Using artificial intelligence – created art to enhance medical education. *American Thoracic Society*, 4(2), pp. 145–151. Available at: https://doi.org/10.34197/ATS-SCHOLAR.2022-0141PS.

Kather, J.N., Ghaffari Laleh, N., Foersch, S. and Truhn, D. (2022) Medical domain knowledge in domain-agnostic generative AI. *NPJ Digital Medicine*, 5(90). Available at: https://doi.org/10.1038/S41746-022-00634-5.

Koljonen, V. (2023) What could we make of AI in plastic surgery education. *Journal of Plastic, Reconstructive and Aesthetic Surgery*, 81, pp. 94–96. Available at: https://doi.org/10.1016/j.bjps.2023.04.055.

Miftahul Amri, M. and Khairatun Hisan, U. (2023) Incorporating AI tools into medical education: Harnessing the benefits of ChatGPT and Dall-E. *Journal of Novel Engineering Science and Technology*, 2(2), pp. 34–39. Available at: https://doi.org/10.56741/JNEST.V2I02.315.

Sarp, S., Kuzlu, M., Wilson, E. and Ozgur, G. (2021) WG2AN: Synthetic wound image generation using generative adversarial network. *The Journal of Engineering*, 5, pp. 286–294. Available at: https://doi.org/10.1049/tje2.12033.

9 Using generative AI agents for scalable roleplay activities in the health sciences

Stian Reimers and Lucy Myers

Introduction

Artificial intelligence is being incorporated rapidly into medical and health sciences practice and training (for a review, see Abd-Alrazaq et al., 2023). In professional practice, it can be used to make more accurate and efficient diagnoses and support medical decision-making (see He et al., 2019); in training, it can be used in simulation to develop students' clinical and communication skills (see Stamer et al., 2023).

We examined the use of generative AI (GenAI) in roleplay activities where an AI agent – here, an AI simulation of a character – takes the role of a key participant in a scenario. Roleplay has a significant part in skills training for health professionals and can be a useful experiential learning tool to develop students' interpersonal and professional skills. Although professional actors are sometimes used, more frequently all roles – patient and clinician – are played by students, which can feel irrelevant or embarrassing, particularly for students playing patients (Stevenson and Sander, 2002). It also requires careful and effortful facilitation. The potential benefits of roleplay are, however, significant. Students get to experience a range of realistic situations and develop communication and judgement skills, flexibility, and confidence, from the interactions.

We looked at using GenAI to play the role of a patient in a complex case scenario. The rationale was twofold: first, to avoid the awkwardness and challenges of students having to play the role of a patient; second, to allow scalability so that multiple groups could engage in the roleplay with limited facilitation.

The aim is not to have a real-time conversation with the AI patient, but to create space to unpack a professional interaction, pausing to explore and discuss potential courses of action at each stage of the conversation with input from students of different disciplines, and subsequently seeing the outcome of those strategies.

DOI: 10.4324/9781003482918-12

Case study: Interprofessional learning

Interprofessional learning in the health sciences, where several professions learn from and about each other to improve professional working, is increasingly included in undergraduate training. We recently developed a series of events where undergraduate students of midwifery, nursing, and speech and language therapy participated in small, interdisciplinary groups, working through activities together.

In one day-long scenario, students engaged with a fictional case study involving a woman, Sarah, who was 38 weeks pregnant at the start of the scenario, with a 9-year-old son who had communication difficulties. The scenario developed over the course of the day, with a number of traditional discursive and analytical activities; the AI-facilitated roleplay activity reported here occurred where Sarah had been discharged after giving birth and was at home being visited by the speech and language therapist.

We built a simple GPT-based roleplay web app using the React and node.js JavaScript frameworks, where groups of students interacted with an AI agent that played the role of Sarah. Building this required a working knowledge of JavaScript and the relevant frameworks, although there are now AI-supported non-coding alternatives, such as OpenAI's freestanding GPTs (https://openai.com/blog/introducing-gpts). The app took typed natural language user input entered into a browser; combined it with a hidden 250-word system prompt providing background and the current scenario, along with any preceding conversation, and high-level instructions for how to respond; and passed it to the OpenAI GPT3.5 API, displaying the response when received.

The 45-minute session comprised 15 groups of 6–10 students, with one facilitator working across several groups. Students were given scenario details and then asked to introduce themselves to 'Sarah' as if they were knocking on her front door. They saw Sarah's response on the screen – in a similar format to a WhatsApp chat – and discussed what approach to take in the next message. The session proceeded in a self-paced manner. In most cases, agreed responses were typed by one student on a computer connected to a projector, although some groups used their own mobile phones.

The system prompt, which gave instructions to the GPT regarding the context, Sarah, and how to respond to different approaches, was not seen by students, so although they knew the details of the scenario, and could see their own submissions and responses from Sarah, they did not know everything about Sarah's current state of mind or preferences. The system prompt was designed to generate discussion about different courses of action: For example, Sarah would not allow the speech and language therapist into her home, so as the interaction developed students discussed whether to be more persistent, try a different approach, or refer to a different agency.

As Sarah's support needs emerged during the roleplay, students discussed how to handle them, and through which professional agency, learning about the resources and support each profession was able to provide as they progressed.

Experience

Although the timescale for implementing the activity meant that we were unable to formally examine student perceptions formally, we were present in around six of the sessions ourselves, where we spoke to around 20 students informally during and after the activity; we also spoke to facilitators of other sessions about their experience.

Feedback based on these informal discussions and observations was generally positive. Unlike traditional roleplay, students showed little embarrassment; the whole group was involved and needed little supervision. Students could choose how involved they wanted to be in discussing and typing; we did not encounter any students who did not want to participate at all. Students liked the open-ended nature of the interaction: They could try different things – ask to hold the baby, ask about the son's well-being – and the AI agent almost always gave appropriate responses, and several described an emotional engagement with 'Sarah' (one midwifery student saying 'I just want to give her a hug'). Students liked working together as a group, having to respond flexibly to developments, and learning about each other's professions.

There was some variability across groups. Where there was less discussion, the task could be completed fairly quickly: one facilitator reported that their conversation fizzled out because the AI Sarah was overly compliant, agreeing with the majority of suggestions. The scenario was also fairly static and lacking in explicit goals so felt a little aimless to some. A more structured, explicitly goal-directed activity could have been more effective overall. Although students liked the novelty of the interaction with an AI agent, they sometimes focused on testing the limits of the system rather than trying to make the best possible responses.

Future development and broader applications

Learning from this initial experience, adjustments to both the prompt and the web app could substantially improve the activity for future students. One development would be to use some simple logic within the web app to change the system prompt fed to the GPT agent: for example, the patient should become distressed or aggressive after a certain period; a new character could arrive at a particular juncture. We are also looking at using the GPT agent to provide automated constructive feedback at the end of the interaction, related to the professionalism of the conversation, the options explored, and overall outcome. We plan to repeat this activity using an updated version of the web app and gathering more formal feedback from students.

We have focused on health sciences, but the potential for AI-based roleplay in higher education is much broader. We have recently started working with our Business School to use a similar approach to negotiation skills training, giving students the opportunity to explore different negotiation strategies with an AI agent before or after applying them to classroom activities. One advantage of using a simple web app to interact with the GPT API is that scenarios can be tweaked or completely changed by editing the system prompt, without the need to alter the code. There is the potential for easily using GenAI for training for a range of professional interactions and decisions with clients, service users, colleagues, and others.

Wider caveats

In developing our activities, we have encountered potential issues with AI-based roleplay that align with more general concerns about the use of GenAI. The first is around the type of character that the AI presents: by default, the system communicates articulately and eloquently, able to explain its own motivation and reasoning, which would usually not capture the range of people that the training would usually seek to build skills with. Essentially by default, it could end up training people to interact effectively with a particular type of introspective, well-educated native English speaker. It is easy enough to add instructions to a prompt specifying the socioeconomic status, neurodiversity, or other properties of the character for the AI to play but then there is the risk that it presents a caricature. This is something that merits scenario-level examination before use.

There are also potential risks around accuracy and bias when the AI agent integrates wider information into its response. In our scenario when asked questions beyond its briefing – the son's communication skills and well-being, or specifics about the home environment – the system usually gave sensible responses that fitted the scenario, as an actor might do. However, when drawing on knowledge outside that given by the scenario, there is again the risk that in addition to potentially including inaccurate information the response reflects its training data, and, hence, predominantly experiences of white, affluent Westerners rather than the range of real patients' experiences (for a broader discussion, see Karabacak et al., 2023).

More generally, we would not recommend replacing existing roleplay or simulated patient activities with AI-based interactions. The experience of interacting with a real person – fellow student, actor, or patient – has many advantages in terms of realism and engagement. However, the scalability, flexibility, and repeatability of AI-based activities mean they can complement face-to-face training by allowing students to explore a wider variety of scenarios, alone or with peers, and consider different approaches to addressing them.

Critical appraisal

Charanjit Sangha, BSc Speech and Language Therapy student, City, University of London

I was a participant in the chatbot patient activity. I thought it was quite novel and modern. It was engaging, and I liked how you couldn't completely predict what it was going to do next or how it would respond to your actions and suggestions, which made it more like the reality of those situations. It made you think on your feet – a useful professional skill – and got us all involved in the task. It encouraged teamwork in deciding roles and pulling in different professions when it looked like they were needed.

We weren't sure of the end goal, and sometimes ended up in cul-de-sacs where the chatbot paused and we weren't sure what to do next. This was quickly overcome when we realised that we could restart it and try again. It was the more tech-savvy people who led initially, but everyone did join in.

I thought it might work better with smaller groups, maybe groups of four rather than our group of eight, with one person from each profession so everyone has to contribute. Having smaller groups completing the activity and then evaluating their different approaches could have been interesting.

Overall, I thought it was an enjoyable, useful activity. It generated an upbeat, informal discussion at the end about what different groups had tried and where they ended up. I think this kind of activity can definitely be run again – particularly with more detailed instructions and aims.

References

Abd-Alrazaq, A., AlSaad, R., Alhuwail, D., Ahmed, A., Healy, P.M., Latifi, S., Damseh, R., Alrazak, S.A. and Sheikh, J. (2023) Large language models in medical education: Opportunities, challenges, and future directions. *JMIR Medical Education*, 9(1), p. e48291. Available at: https://doi.org/10.2196/48291.

He, J., Baxter, S.L., Xu, J., Xu, J., Zhou, X. and Zhang, K. (2019) The practical implementation of artificial intelligence technologies in medicine. *Nature Medicine*, 25(1), pp. 30–36. Available at: https://doi.org/10.1038/s41591-018-0307-0.

Karabacak, M., Ozkara, B.B., Margetis, K., Wintermark, M. and Bisdas, S. (2023) The advent of generative language models in medical education. *JMIR Medical Education*, 9, p. e48163. Available at: https://doi.org/10.2196/48163.

Stamer, T., Steinhäuser, J. and Flägel, K. (2023) Artificial intelligence supporting the training of communication skills in the education of health care professions: Scoping review. *Journal of Medical Internet Research*, 25, p. e43311. Available at: https://doi.org/10.2196/43311.

Stevenson, K. and Sander, P. (2002) Medical students are from Mars-business and psychology students are from Venus-University teachers are from Pluto? *Medical Teacher*, 24(1), pp. 27–31. Available at: https://doi.org/10.1080/00034980120103441.

10 Embracing GenAI in education

A path towards authentic assessment

Noelle Hatley and Pauline Penny

Introduction

University education aims to foster meaningful engagement with the world (Ashwin, 2023). One way of doing this is through authentic assessment, by focusing on the authenticity of the task, and its relevance to society (McArthur, 2022). This way students are supported in becoming part of a larger community and enriching their sense of achievement, self-esteem, and well-being.

Aligning with Department for Education guidelines (DFE, 2023), students can develop knowledge and intellectual capabilities to utilise GenAI technology within a seminar, safely and effectively. If used ethically and intelligently, GenAI has the potential to support learning and prepare students for future work (Manchester Metropolitan University (MMU, 2023a).

The first module plays a pivotal role in introducing and guiding students into higher education, acquainting them with the subject matter, developing effective study methods, and cultivating a positive experience. This case study illustrates how GenAI can assist students without compromising research integrity or academic standards. It modifies the assessment brief for authentic assessment, addressing the challenge of comprehensively covering the broad topic of the global fashion industry, and helping students meet learning outcomes. In the past, the breadth of the unit topic has sometimes led to them struggling to find a starting point, or to create a plan that enables them to meet the ratified learning outcomes.

Authentic assessment and GenAI

McArthur (2022) proposes a new way of looking at authentic assessment that considers its social impact believing that this approach can help students develop more meaningful and relevant skills and knowledge that can benefit themselves and the society. GenAI already assists with scaffolding and application in the workplace (Umutlu and Gursoy, 2022), for example, to analyse and derive insights from large data sets. A revised assessment brief and

DOI: 10.4324/9781003482918-13

the introduction of GenAI enhanced the authenticity of the module and its assessment.

Research by Janschitz and Penker (2022) highlights the significant variability in the degree of digitalisation among students typically classified as 'Digital Natives'. This variation underscores that not all young people are equally digitally competent; therefore, the aim was to encourage experimentation, offer guidance, and explore the limitations of ChatGPT-3.5 to align with students' learning behaviour and demonstrate potential risks. Understanding the limitations of GenAI in academia is crucial. ChatGPT-3.5 (Open AI Chat GPT-3.5, 2023) acknowledges issues like generating false information, bias, inappropriate content, and inconsistent responses. It emphasises the need for caution and critical thinking in academic and research contexts.

In module planning, ethical considerations such as the risk of personal data being shared were critical. The university does not currently support ChatGPT-3.5 so students were not required to sign up, instead, teaching staff with existing accounts demonstrated its usage. More details are shown in the seminar activity section.

Assessment brief

The revised module design aimed to support the hypothesis that the use of GenAI proactively combined with an updated assessment brief, can maintain academic integrity, and enhance student understanding, thus supporting McArthur's broader view of authentic assessment.

The Global Fashion Industry module is in the first semester and introduces first-year fashion business students from three different programmes to the broader fashion industry. The learning outcomes were unchanged, but revisions were made to the assessment brief and the teaching schedule as described below.

The assessment

The previous format was divided into subject-specific sections comprising of the global market, the competition, the consumer, and global issues, whereas the new format is in two parts: Part 1 – academic model (PESTEL). Part 2 – table that summarised findings in relation to the learning outcomes (LO's). The assessment brief also stipulates a minimum number of credible sources to ensure academic integrity (JCQ, 2023). These adjustments increased the level of resilience to inappropriate use of GenAI as students must demonstrate an understanding of material by analysing it from two distinctly different perspectives. It also simplifies how work is assessed as marks are distributed across two sections, the Pestel and the LO table, rather than three sections previously.

Table 10.1 Unit assessment structure: considering authentic assessment and GenAI (ChatGPT-3.5 GPT)

Level 4 (First-Year) Assessment Report Structure

2022/23 Assessment Brief	2023/24 Assessment Brief	Authentic assessment/GenAI/ Academic integrity
Introduction	Introduction	n/a
(Section 1.) The Global Market	Part 1. PESTEL model about the Global Fashion Industry.	Using an analytical model to answer a specific question requires students to manipulate information from a range of different sources and synthesise into one response. The topic of research through a PESTEL serves to demonstrate societal trends and to improve the authenticity of the assessment. While GenAI could be used to help research the topics academic integrity is maintained through the quality of referencing required.
(Section 2.) Competition	Part 2. Table that summarises findings in relation to the learning outcomes.	Finding and utilising information from a range of credible academic sources to describe how they have met the unit learning outcomes requires students to collect and apply information in response to different stimuli.
(Section 3. Global issues	Conclusion	n/a.
Conclusion	See above	
References	References. Minimum of 12 stipulated.	Stipulating a minimum of 12 credible sources encourages students ChatGPT-3.5 to find, cite, and reference the original source of information.

Sources of information

In response to GenAI's unreliability of information and inability to provide reliable sources for information generated, the assessment brief stipulated that a minimum of 12 credible academic sources must be used. It is important to note that the expectation is that the tabulation of learnings against the LO's will lead to a reduction in marking time, allowing time to be spent verifying the 12 references.

Seminar activity

In the week, three seminar students evaluated ChatGPT-3.5. To avoid ethical issues involving data breaches, students were not requested to sign up to it, instead, handouts from previously generated responses to 'What are the main issues in the global fashion industry' were provided. In the second stage, students suggested questions which tutors input into Chat GPT-3.5 and shared the responses on screen. In the final two stages, students did their own research from academic sources through the library comparing findings from both sources. They highlighted many of the expected issues: unreliability, missing references, and broken URL links. Table 10.2 summarises the four seminar stages.

It was emphasised to all students that if they independently used any GenAI, they must reference in accordance with MMU guidelines.

Results and discussion

At the beginning of the seminar, students were asked what they knew about ChatGPT. 93% of the 115 students who responded had never heard of it or heard of it but never used it. This was a significant number indicating a lower level of awareness than anticipated. See Figure 10.1.

Table 10.2 Summary of week 3 seminar

Week 3 seminar activity

Stage 1	Handouts provided to students of a range of generated content relating to the assignment from ChatGPT-3.5.
Stage 2	Students suggest further assignment-related questions. Staff share ChatGPT-3.5 responses on screen.
Stage 3	Students do independent research from credible academic sources to evaluate the content generated from ChatGPT-3.5 and reference appropriately.
Stage 4	Students reflect on the success of ChatGPT-3.5 in relation to meeting the module learning outcomes.

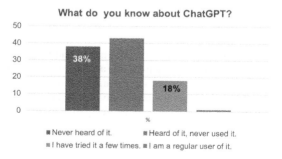

Figure 10.1 Student awareness of ChatGPT at the beginning of the seminar.

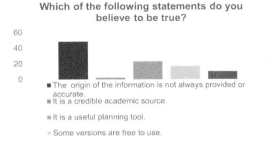

Which of the following statements do you believe to be true?

- The origin of the information is not always provided or accurate.
- It is a credible academic source.
- It is a useful planning tool.
- Some versions are free to use.

Figure 10.2 Student perception of ChatGPT at the end of the seminar.

It was important to develop student understanding of how ChatGPT can be used, so a further question was asked at the end of the seminar (multiple options could be selected). The most common response (48%) was that the origin of the information was not always provided or accurate. 23% highlighted that ChatGPT could be a useful planning tool. See Figure 2. These findings aligned with our seminar objectives.

The data collected at the end of the seminar established that this year in The Global Fashion Industry first-year unit students were cautious about using GenAI other than to assist with planning. Module assignments are due mid-December, after which further analysis of student work, specifically how they have used GenAI will be completed.

Conclusion

The introduction of GenAI in this module was in response to increased concern in academia about the use of generative AI platforms in relation to trust, transparency, and accountability (Vincent-Lancrin and van der Vlies, 2020). It was also an opportunity to increase the authenticity of the assignment. The findings were that students were less aware of GenAI than expected, but that by the end of the seminar could highlight its limitations. While this provided invaluable experience for the students, some modifications will be made before repeating the activity. The proposal for next year's curriculum situates the seminar in week 7, capitalising on heightened student engagement in sourcing information, given its proximity to the assignment submission deadline. The shift to Bing Chat GenAI, supported by MMU (2023b), rather than ChatGPT reflects a commitment to ethical considerations.

Assignments are submitted mid-December, at which point, lessons learned from the influence of ChatGPT will be drawn and used to inform future module planning, and more broadly across the faculty. Further developments in this fast-moving field will require HE to constantly review policies and assessments to provide the best experience for students while preparing them for life after university. In this context, ethical considerations and sustainability will remain paramount in shaping the trajectory of AI integration within academic settings.

Critical appraisal

Julie Hodson, programme leader, fashion business and management, fashion marketing, fashion buying, and merchandising. Manchester Metropolitan University
The case study evaluates integrating GenAI, ChatGPT-3.5, within a first-year fashion business module at Manchester Metropolitan University (MMU), focusing on authentic assessment. It responds to evolving educational needs by preparing students for emerging technologies.

Strengths lie in its relevance to changing educational paradigms and emphasis on authentic assessment. Ethical considerations, including data protection and information reliability, are evident. The study actively engages students in critical evaluation of GenAI usage through seminar activities.

However, limitations arise from the inability to directly align GenAI use with ratified learning outcomes, restricting its broader application. Initial student awareness gaps suggest a need for improved communication regarding GenAI's relevance. Evaluation relies on student perceptions, lacking robust metrics.

In summary, while the study showcases innovative GenAI integration with a focus on authenticity and ethics, the inability to directly link it with ratified learning outcomes presents a challenge. Improved communication strategies and comprehensive assessment methods are crucial for evaluating its impact across diverse educational domains without altering established learning objectives.

References

Ashwin, P. (2023). What could it take to build a transformational learning community? Manchester Met Learning and Teaching Conference 2023, Building a Transformational Active Learning Community. https://www.utaresources.mmu.ac.uk/leed-conference-23/#/programme
Department for Education (DFE) (2023) *Generative Artificial Intelligence in Education. Departmental Statement. DfE External Document Template.* Available at: https://dera.ioe.ac.uk/id/eprint/39800/1/Generative_artificial_intelligence_in_education_.pdf (Accessed 11 July 2023).
Janschitz, G. and Penker, M. (2022) How digital are 'digital natives' actually? Developing an instrument to measure the degree of digitalisation of university students – the DDS-Index. *Bulletin of Sociological Methodology/Bulletin de Méthodologie Sociologique*, 153(1), pp. 127–159. Available at: https://doi.org/10.1177/07591063211061760.

Joint Council for Qualifications (JCQ) (2023) *AI Use in Assessments: Protecting the Integrity of Qualifications.* Available at: www.jcq.org.uk/examsoffice/malpractice/artificial-intelligence/ (Accessed 23 August 2023).

McArthur, J. (2022) Rethinking authentic assessment: Work, well-being, and society. *Higher Education*, 85, pp. 8–101. Available at: https://doi.org/10.1007/s10734-022-00822-y.

MMU (2023a) *GenAI & ChatGPT-3.5GPT. Manchester Met Intranet.* Available at: mmu.ac.uk (Accessed 21 August 2023).

MMU (2023b) *Generative AI in Education: Staff Guidance. Manchester Met Intranet.* Available at: mmu.ac.uk (Accessed 8 November 23).

Open AI Chat GPT-3.5 (2023) Chat GPT-3.5 response to Noelle Hatley, (personal communication 21 August 2023). Available at: https://chat.openai.com/.

Umutlu, D. and Gursoy, M.E. (2022) Leveraging artificial intelligence techniques for effective scaffolding of personalized learning in workplaces. *Artificial Intelligence Education in the Context of Work*, pp. 59–76. Available at: https://doi.org/10.1007/978-3-031-14489-9_4.

Vincent-Lancrin, S. and van der Vlies, R. (2020) Trustworthy artificial intelligence (AI) in education: Promises and challenges. In *OECD Education Working Papers, No. 218.* Paris: OECD Publishing. Available at: https://doi.org/10.1787/a6c90fa9-en.

Part D

Assessment in a generative AI-enabled world

11 Generative AI and the implications for authentic assessment

Stephen Powell and Rachel Forsyth

Authentic assessment

The term authentic assessment (AA), as with many educational concepts, is a malleable one and, for the purpose of this chapter, it is not necessary to define a precise meaning. Adapted to a higher education context, an AA has been defined by Villarroel et al. (2018) as one set in a realistic and rich societal context, which represents a worthwhile task, perhaps involving external stakeholders, and requiring higher-order skills to undertake. It is clear that a task which can be quickly completed by the simple use of a digital aid such as a GenAI tool could not meet this definition.

The benefits of authentic assessment for both students and society are well recognised (McArthur, 2023; Swaffield, 2011). McArthur also highlights the lack of a philosophical basis for the use of the term authentic, but identifies that publications about the topic are generally focused on the interests of the student. Three core ideas put forward by McArthur (2023, p. 87) include:

1. 'to shift our focus from the real world/world of work to a richer understanding of society as a whole;
2. secondly, to transcend a focus simply on the task, and consider instead the value of that task; and
3. . . . outline an understanding of authentic assessment which does not reinforce the status-quo but is instead a vehicle for transformative social change'.

In explaining the three points above, McArthur seeks to put the student at the centre of the task, but within the context of the wider society in which they live and work. In point three, this is taken a step further with the idea of the transformation of society, which could include the workplace, rather than simply an ability to respond to changes brought about by wider societal and economic shifts. In addition, Ashwin (2023) and McArthur underscore the importance of discipline and subject as the foundation for knowledge and skills that prepare individuals to fully participate in societal change. These

DOI: 10.4324/9781003482918-15

ideas resonate well with Biesta's (2020) three 'purposes' of education, *qualification* which is a measure of the knowledge and skills gained by students, *socialisation* which can be thought of as the joining of a community of practitioners with all of the complexity that entails, and lastly *subjectification*, which can be thought of as a 'who are the students becoming'. It is this last purpose which seems to us to connect most strongly with the richer proposal of AA put forward by McArthur as it encapsulates how a student will choose to interact and engage with society. Ajjawi et al. (2023) suggest that it is not possible, or necessary, to design authenticity into every assignment task, but that a continuing focus on developing evaluative judgement of authenticity in all assignments will help to prepare students for a world which changes rapidly, including the availability of GenAI tools.

Designing worthwhile and relevant assessments is a challenge for teachers. One way to develop authentic and engaging ways of assessing requires students to be involved in the creation of the curriculum and its assessment so that it is felt to be authentic not just by the teachers but also by those who participate in the assessment. There can be no one blueprint for curriculum co-creation, but a simple and workable definition by Bovill et al. (2016, p. 196) is 'co-creation of learning and teaching occurs when staff and students work collaboratively with one another to create components of curricula and/ or pedagogical approaches'. With no student involvement, the authenticity or not of an assessment rests solely with the academic, making it susceptible to their personal biases. Students can get involved by talking about how an assignment links to their own experiences, reflecting on what they learned by doing the task, practising self or peer assessment using the marking criteria, and explaining how they acted on the feedback they received.

We have set out above a view of AA and, through a suggested approach of co-creation, a way of ensuring assessments are felt to be authentic by teachers and their students. GenAI has a supporting role to play in AA when used knowingly by students as a way of tackling the task, getting personalised help, comparing outcomes, and making critical judgements. To achieve this, rather than a focus just on the product, our assessment design and marking criteria should make transparent the thought processes of the student in using the GenAI through reflection, analysis, and evaluative judgments informing planning for future study or work. It is these higher-order skills that we should assess.

Assessment design

The assessment lifecycle (Forsyth et al., 2015) is an established way of looking at assessment design, valuing each part of the assessment process. We have selected five key stages to examine in relation to the potential use of GenAI tools: setting, supporting, marking, providing feedback, and reflecting.

Setting

GenAI tools present both challenges and opportunities to conventional assessment in higher education. These challenges stem from the need to ensure the validity of the assessment (does it test our intended learning outcomes?) and its security (how can we be sure that the student achieved the learning outcomes in the way we intended?) (Dawson, 2020). The opportunities, which will no doubt be highly disputed, may lie in improved access to idea generation and well-written outputs for all students.

Validity

Many different tasks can demonstrate that students have achieved a particular learning outcome. These outcomes typically revolve around three key components: an initial action verb identifying the desired behaviour, a subject specifying the area of application, and a final context constraining the scope of what needs to be demonstrated so that it is not too broad to be achieved. For instance, if the learning outcome is 'Plan a communication strategy for a proposed organisational improvement based on your enquiry', then the students could be asked to produce an annotated bibliography, an oral presentation, a video, or a poster (among other possibilities), to suit the audience. Generative AI tools can support the student by helping them to find suitable literature, perhaps providing more interesting search criteria than would be found in conventional database search tools – for instance 'find me articles published on communications strategies in family-owned businesses/large multinationals/charitable organisations' or 'find me articles which show ways to communicate organisational improvements in marketing/accounting/customer relations'. Equally, that learning outcome could be assessed as part of a larger piece of work like an essay or research report, alongside other outcomes like 'synthesise literature into a coherent review' and 'report results in a way which is suitable for your peers'. GenAI tools can give the students feedback on the structure and quality of writing in the finished document.

Security

The second of these questions is the one which has probably concerned people most in relation to assessment and GenAI: How do we know that the student did the work themselves? This is not a new question: whenever there is a high-stakes assessment, students will be anxious about their performance, and some may look for ways to take shortcuts, GenAI advantage, or deceive the examiner. The difference now is that GenAI tools produce plausible output very quickly, which may make all of these actions easier and cheaper.

When designing an assessment think: What are the students expected to demonstrate? Is it that they can complete an entire process by themselves without reference to any external resources (books, web pages, course notes, etc.)? Should they complete the task in a fixed time? If so, the assignment task should be a controlled examination, where the conditions under which students address the question are constrained. Examples of this type of assessment which might fit the 'authentic' label would be clinical or practical examinations, or some types of oral examinations such as mock interviews.

Maintaining authenticity

However, there are few AAs which we would want to constrain in these ways. If we take Villaroel et al.'s definition of AAs being set in a rich societal context, then we expect students to have access to a range of resources while they are working on these assignment tasks. We probably want them to learn how to reflect on a piece of work, revise it, have it peer reviewed, and feel that they have created a meaningful final submission. We have to consider, during the design, that they will now have access to GenAI tools and that this may change our expectations of the product they submit for assessment. It may be that there is a need to return to the learning outcomes to ensure that they capture what students should demonstrate, if they are now working with generally available GenAI tools. As an example, take a generic learning outcome:

> Analyse key issues of professional argument, debate or controversy of broad interest within your chosen field of practice in debate with other students.

This could be adapted to:

> Analyse key issues of professional argument, debate or controversy of broad interest within your chosen field of practice in debate with other students, *explaining the sources and validity of your arguments*.

A way to deal with this is to expect transparency, so that the student declares what they have used and how, for instance, 'I used ChatGPT to produce computer code to run the analysis presented here'. If this is replacing work previously expected of the students, then they need to do something else. This is an opportunity to assess higher-order thinking skills. They could be asked to explain how they checked the quality and accuracy of the outputs from the GenAI tool, or what they gained (or lost) in terms of understanding from using the tools and how they might do things differently in the future. Or a written product could be supplemented with a short in-person or online oral examination using probing questions to check understanding.

Supporting

If GenAI tools are part of the skills students need to develop, then they can be incorporated into classroom activities, such as the following:

Idea generation – using a GenAI tool to suggest ways to tackle the set assignment task, or what kinds of topics to look for in a literature search.

Output critique – generating some outputs on a topic related to the assignment and talking about what grade such output would get. This has the added benefit of encouraging discussion about criteria and what wants students should learn.

Structuring – get each student to bring a structure for the assignment task to class which has been generated by a GenAI tool and discuss its quality. Or ask them to write their own structure under supervision and then see what a GenAI tool suggests, and compare.

'Shut up and write' – get everyone to write a paragraph for their assignment under examination-type conditions in class, and then peer review them. Questions could be 'What is good about the paragraphs? How would you edit it? What does this teach you about writing for this assignment and my expectations?'

Literature search – give a literature search task, either the same for all or different ones for different groups (or let them make their own related to the assignment), and use different GenAI tools to find literature. Discuss the outputs and compare them with the library catalogue and search tools. A bonus is to involve a librarian in this activity. They may find that the results from the GenAI tools are disappointing. For instance, in September 2023, we searched for papers on 'authentic assessment'. The most recent was from 2017!

GenAI tools will improve, and the outputs from these tasks will change, but they will remain valid because they rely on students understanding what they are receiving in the way of outputs and how to make critical judgements about them.

Marking

If the assignment task will include reflections on process, or critique of the tools used to produce the work, then the marking criteria will need to change. Table 11.1 shows one simple approach, which can be readily adapted for a range of learning outcomes.

Providing feedback

If the marking criteria have been adapted, then so will be the feedback strategy: the possible or declared use of GenAI tools can be dealt with as would

Table 11.1 Ideas for adapting marking criteria when GenAI tools may have been used ('previous' examples from Forsyth, 2022)

Level	Previous criterion for a pass	New criterion
First-year undergraduate/ bachelors	Information from primary and secondary sources is collected and applied to authentic problems under supervision.	Information from primary and secondary sources is collected and applied to authentic problems under supervision. The source validity is evaluated, including the use or potential use of GenAI tools.
Second-year undergraduate/ bachelors	A simple project is designed and carried out to collect, analyse, and critique information from primary and secondary sources in a realistic context under supervision.	A simple project is designed and carried out to collect, analyse, and critique information from primary and secondary sources in a realistic context under supervision. The source validity is evaluated and compared with historical approaches.
Third-year undergraduate/ bachelors	A complex authentic project is designed, planned, and carried out using an appropriate range of primary and secondary sources. The results and/ or outcomes are evaluated accurately.	A complex authentic project is designed, planned, and carried out using an appropriate range of primary and secondary sources. The results and/or outcomes are evaluated accurately with full consideration of the quality of the tools used or rejected, including GenAI tools.
Masters	A professional project is planned and carried out to gather information from appropriate primary and secondary sources and synthesise the results.	A professional project is planned and carried out to gather information from appropriate primary and secondary sources and synthesise the results. The use of GenAI tools is considered and critiqued in relation to the project.

with any other tool used to support preparation of the assignment. Table 11.2 shows some sample phrases which further emphasise the need for taking responsibility for the use of the tools.

Reviewing

The assessment lifecycle ends with a review of the task as a whole. As part of this, it is natural to review any changes, such as the introduction of GenAI tools.

Table 11.2 Some sample feedback comments which assume that GenAI tools have been used

---

I did not see any form of GenAI tool referred to in your analysis – these tools are now frequently used for this kind of task, so even if you did not choose to use them, I would expect to see some mention of your reasoning in the analysis.

Your explanation of how you used GenAI tools was insightful and interesting – I learned something from it myself, particularly how you developed your skill to input instructions (data wrangling!).

In future assignments, could you consider using a GenAI tool such as XXX to extend the range of references you found?

You need to be more critical of the use of GenAI tools in this field – this is not sufficiently analytical. Ask yourself questions such as 'Why are human interactions important in this context and what is the difference between GenAI output and a conversation with a peer?'; 'How do I judge the quality of output from a GenAI tool? What reference points should I use?'

You made sensible recommendations for the customer based on a limited analysis of their situation. In your next assignment, consider whether you can offer a wider range of possibilities, taking into account their future needs as well as their current ones. You could try asking a GenAI tool to generate ideas about future needs.

It should be possible to compare previous years' performance with the new ones – Has the use of GenAI tools had any impact on student performance? Have any gaps between different groups been reduced, or increased: Did everyone get an equal chance to achieve? What do students say about the assignment and their use of GenAI tools? This leads back to the beginning of the lifecycle, making incremental changes, or even rejecting the use of GenAI tools.

Key points for educational developers

The availability of generative AI tools places even greater emphasis on the need for a clear understanding of assessment design principles, and an opportunity to work with students towards more AA. In this chapter, we have suggested some simple ways to design assessments in the age of AI, based on established existing approaches and principles:

1. Work with students and/or potential employers to identify AA opportunities.
2. Review learning outcomes to ensure that assessment tasks are still valid and secure when GenAI tools are available.
3. Review grading criteria and feedback plan to reflect the possible use of GenAI tools.

Conclusion

An intentional move to AA shifts focus from the judgement of a finished product to an engagement and evaluation of the processes which led to that product. This provides opportunities to make constructive use of GenAI tools in all aspects of the assessment lifecycle, from creating case studies and exemplars through idea forming, literature searches, structuring submissions, marking, and feedback. It is also important to consider the ethical, environmental, and academic benefits and disadvantages: these options may not always be desirable, and it is important for those who support academics to understand the full range of possibilities in order to advise their colleagues effectively.

Critical appraisal

Dr Peter Gossman, University of Worcester
I am a postgraduate certificate tutor for a course in teaching higher education teachers/lecturers. In this role, I have grappled with AA and what this means for the course participants. When AI burst onto the landscape a year or so ago, I wondered if it could produce a nice reflection piece that fulfilled the requirements of the assessments for the Post Graduate Certificate. Of course, it can. However, I am at pains to stress to my colleagues/peers who are taking the course that the point is for them to become better, more knowledgeable, more scholarly, more . . . (what I hope for is that their learners learn because of their teacher rather than despite them). If an AI writes the assignment the above is probably not taking place, certainly, they are not reflecting if the AI is doing it for them.

The natural extension is now to explore how AI can add to authenticity. In the near future, HE teachers will be drawing upon its fantastic potential to develop and enhance their own teaching. Reading this chapter will provide a strong starting point for anyone thinking about the advice they give to academics and their institution about how to integrate AI as part of business as usual and why it is important to think seriously about not just how, but what we are seeking to develop in individuals through assessment.

References

Ajjawi, R., Tai, J., Dollinger, M., Dawson, P., Boud, D. and Bearman, M. (2023) From authentic assessment to authenticity in assessment: Broadening perspectives. *Assessment & Evaluation in Higher Education*, 1–12. Available at: https://doi.org/10.1080/02602938.2023.2271193.

Ashwin, P. (2023) What could it take to build a transformational learning community? [Paper presentation] *Manchester Met Teaching and Learning Conference*, 14 June 2023.

Biesta, G. (2020) Risking ourselves in education: Qualification, socialization, and subjectification revisited. *Educational Theory*, 70, pp. 89–104. Available at: https://onlinelibrary.wiley.com/doi/10.1111/edth.12411.

Bovill, C., Cook-Sather, A., Felten, P., Millard, L. and Moore-Cherry, N. (2016) Addressing potential challenges in co-creating learning and teaching: Overcoming resistance, navigating institutional norms and ensuring inclusivity in student – staff partnerships. *Higher Education*, 71(2), pp. 195–208. Available at: https://doi.org/10.1007/s10734-015-9896-4.

Dawson, P. (2020) *Defending Assessment Security in a Digital World: Preventing e-Cheating and Supporting Academic Integrity in Higher Education.* London: Routledge. ISBN9780429324178.

Forsyth, R. (2022) *Confident Assessment in Higher Education.* London: SAGE. ISBN-10:1529770807.

Forsyth, R., Cullen, R., Ringan, N. and Stubbs, M. (2015) Supporting the development of assessment literacy of staff through institutional process change. *London Review of Education*, 13, pp. 34–41. Available at: https://uclpress.scienceopen.com/hosted-document?doi=10.18546/LRE.13.3.05.

McArthur, J. (2023) Rethinking authentic assessment: Work, well-being, and society. *Higher Education*, 85(1), pp. 85–101. Available at: https://doi.org/10.1007/s10734-022-00822-y.

Swaffield, S. (2011) Getting to the heart of authentic assessment for learning. *Assessment in Education: Principles, Policy & Practice*, 18(4), pp. 433–449. Available at: https://doi.org/10.1080/0969594X.2011.582838.

Villarroel, V., Bloxham, S., Bruna, D., Bruna, C. and Herrera-Seda, C. (2018) Authentic assessment: Creating a blueprint for course design. *Assessment & Evaluation in Higher Education*, 43(5), pp. 840–854. Available at: https://doi.org/10.1080/02602938.2017.1412396.

12 Embracing generative AI in authentic assessment

Challenges, ethics, and opportunities

Rebecca Upsher, Claire Heard, Sumeyra Yalcintas, Jayne Pearson, and James Findon

Introduction

Generative artificial intelligence (GenAI) is increasingly recognised for its ability to revolutionise and automate work-related tasks across a wide array of contexts, such as data analysis and decision-making (Chui et al., 2023). Therefore, incorporating GenAI into higher education (HE) curricula is essential in providing students opportunities to explore and experiment with this technology, fostering the development of GenAI-ready professionals who can capably harness the potential of GenAI in their future careers and members of society. This can be achieved through authentic assessment.

Authentic assessments are designed to closely mirror real-world tasks in an applied setting, providing students with a more realistic and meaningful context in which to apply their knowledge and skills (Janesick, 2006). In the context of GenAI, this may involve projects where students experiment with GenAI tools to solve real-world problems in their field of study. As educators, ignoring GenAI is not the answer. Yet, responding to this changing landscape by blanketly embracing GenAI into assessment to retain societal relevance and authenticity has its challenges. Among these challenges are the potential impacts on the future workforce and wider societal view, upholding standards of academic integrity, ensuring inclusive assessment, and addressing concerns of digital equality.

This chapter offers a critical exploration of these challenges and presents opportunities associated with incorporating GenAI in the context of authentic assessment in a meaningful and responsible way (Bankins and Formosa, 2023; McArthur, 2023). This chapter extends beyond merely preparing students for the world of work, reaching into broader implications for academia and society.

Challenges and ethics

Implications for the future workforce and wider societal view

Limited guidance on GenAI use might disadvantage students. Over-reliance risks a lack of proper GenAI safety etiquette, with students sharing data with

DOI: 10.4324/9781003482918-16

GenAI platforms without discerning data protection and intellectual property implications. This could also foster a culture of laziness (Ahmad et al., 2023) and over-reliance on GenAI, possibly producing under-skilled graduates. Lower-order thinking tasks, like factual recall, are vulnerable to GenAI. Such tasks, even before the rise of GenAI, do not foster deep-learning approaches and often lead to surface-level learning approaches that seldom aid students in their careers (Biggs and Tang, 2007). In contrast, higher-order tasks, encompassing skills such as decision-making, interpersonal communication, and meta-cognition, are less AI vulnerable. These skills are increasingly seen as essential for the future workforce as more routine tasks face automation (Langreo, 2023).

However, McArthur (2016) argues that employability-focused education and assessment have the potential to see students as products or outputs with little agency to change the world in which they live, advocating that true authentic assessment must be intrinsically meaningful in its own right. An assessment task should be seen as valuable, not necessarily in its output but through the process of doing that task. In calling for this reframing of authenticity, McArthur (2023) asks us to consider what it means to be human, to recognise the relationship between self and society, and where change can be affected. It is this concept that we argue here is crucial to any attempt to embed GenAI into assessment strategies in HE. Assessment is often 'performed on' students (Boud, 2000, p. 156), constraining their sense of intrinsic meaning and emphasising output for a grade, judged by standards external to themselves. By embracing the core principles of authentic and meaningful assessment, this provides the opportunity to champion 'assessment for learning' over 'assessment of learning' (Sambell et al., 2012, p. 3). Furthermore, there have been calls for a focus on 'sustainable' assessment which allows students to meet their own future learning needs (Boud and Soler, 2016), by aligning with principles of assessment for learning. By involving students in the assessment process in various ways, they are better able to develop confidence in themselves as agents of change in the world. Assessment, therefore, should facilitate agency, not only in the tasks that are set but also in the process of their completion.

Academic integrity

Academic integrity is a broad term that can be open to different interpretations (Macfarlane et al., 2014). Here, we define academic integrity as referring to issues relating to student academic (mis)conduct. Academic integrity is an essential principle in academia and all members of the academic community are expected to uphold and adhere to scholarly standards. These standards include the originality of the student's own work, the accurate attribution of sources, and the appropriate collection and use of data. There is evidence that both students and staff perceive GenAI to be a potential threat to academic integrity (Chan, 2023). It is therefore important to review the challenges posed by GenAI in the context of academic integrity.

A central pillar of academic integrity is the requirement for students to produce original work and avoid plagiarism or misrepresenting the work of others as their own. This can be unintentionally or intentionally contravened by copying the work of others (students or academics) or by omitting proper attribution to sources.

While it is evident that internet-based similarity detection services and staff show a limited capacity to distinguish GenAI-assisted writing, with detection rates approximately at 53–54% (Khalil and Er, 2023; Perkins et al., 2023), this should not be the sole focus of our response to GenAI in academic settings. The approach should not just be reactively using tools against potential misuse of GenAI but also proactive strategies that enhance the learning process. This will help promote authentic assessment and evaluate the learning journey rather than just the end result or the capabilities of GenAI. Furthermore, there is a risk of damaging the student–teacher relationship if the focus shifts to over-policing student work and presuming a propensity to cheat. Nurturing a positive educational environment is as important as the technical aspects of combating GenAI misuse. Therefore, authentic assessment is not only a response to a challenge but also an opportunity to enrich learning during the age of GenAI.

Inclusive assessment

There has been a reaction among some academics to return to measures that ensure academic integrity, such as mass in-person exams and Vivas. However, as McArthur (2016) points out, these assessments can contribute to the exclusion of students with particular characteristics. For example, in-person exams often disadvantage students with specific learning disabilities, due to social conditions like lack of peer support, and material conditions such as unsuitable exam environments and inadequate access to necessary resources (Tai et al., 2023). Even when procedures are put in place to mitigate these disadvantages, there can still be a sense of social stigma felt by students (Waterfield and West, 2008). Indeed, the use of exams as a response to GenAI has been discouraged by the Russell Group or universities (2023).

The suggestion of widespread use of Vivas as a means to ensure originality of students' work (Dobson, 2023) is fraught with issues for students with social anxiety and for international students. There have been calls for caution in the use of oral assessments more generally following the tragic case of Natasha Abrahart, a physics student who took her own life in 2018. This incident occurred after she was required to participate in an oral exam, despite the university being aware of her severe social anxiety (Dickinson, 2022).

There is no single assessment that is inherently inclusive. For assessment to be inclusive, flexibility, rather than restriction of assessment types and processes is required, although there is tension between this and the desire to ensure academic integrity while maintaining standards. Embracing AI, however, still poses challenges for inclusive assessment. Some GenAI tools have been shown to produce biased outputs in terms of gender and racial stereotypes (Nkonde, 2023). Large language models (LLMs) are trained on freely available data, largely English and Western epistemologies, with results that often exclude or misrepresent the contribution of People of Colour and perspectives from the Global South (Ferrara, 2023). Students and staff with high critical digital literacy and/or social justice concerns may be aware of this and may choose not to use such technologies as a protest against the way that such bias can be perpetuated. It is important to allow choice in AI use for students. The current approach taken by universities whose statements are publicly available is to allow students to use GenAI within certain parameters but not to require its use. It can be argued, however, that GenAI has been a catalyst for recognising some of these concerns and strengthening the calls across the sector for conversations around decolonisation and embedding critical digital literacy in the curriculum. Despite these challenges, GenAI's potential to address broader educational inequalities cannot be overlooked.

Digital inequality

GenAI holds the potential to diminish digital and other societal inequalities. For instance, it could assist those with disabilities to enhance their learning experience, bridge language gaps among students (Božić, 2023), and democratise knowledge more broadly (Lim et al., 2023). Consequently, the integration of GenAI into curricula can encourage inclusive approaches and equalise assessment conditions.

Nevertheless, GenAI can also exacerbate digital inequality. The GenAI digital divide encompasses unequal access to GenAI tools and the internet (the GenAI digital divide), coupled with insufficient training (GenAI literacy) (Božić, 2023). It further amplifies the economic gap between individuals who can afford premium GenAI software subscriptions with advanced features and those who rely on the free versions (Božić, 2023). Academic institutions must be vigilant about these issues.

For instance, when introducing GenAI training to students, it is essential to use freely accessible versions and platforms with safe data privilege policies. This promotes responsible GenAI development and ensures equitable access. It is also a step towards equipping individuals with the skills to confidently navigate the evolving AI landscape.

Consisting as a subset of digital literacy, GenAI literacy refers to understanding and evaluating AI outputs, as well as mastering 'Prompt Engineering', the skill of effectively crafting AI inputs (Lim et al., 2023). Beyond understanding content generation, it encompasses recognising biases and ethical considerations. A GenAI literacy deficit could lead to misconceptions about data privacy, biases, and ethical implications (Chan and Hu, 2023). As students and staff engage more with AI systems, enhancing GenAI literacy is crucial to enhance its potential and for responsible and ethical AI utilisation, alongside other learning activities that teach more general digital literacy skills.

To navigate the challenges of integrating GenAI into authentic assessment, the following 'Opportunities Checklist' highlights key opportunities and offers guidance for educators.

Opportunities checklist

Below is a checklist of opportunities to consider when designing GenAI-integrated authentic assessments, highlighting distinct opportunities presented by GenAI, and broader, non-AI-specific principles that have emerged in the field of HE assessment in response to the rise of AI technologies.

1. **Focus on the process over the outcome:** By encouraging students to concentrate more on the learning process, such as developing metacognitive skills, we can help them view GenAI as a tool for learning enhancement rather than as a means to shortcut the intended outcome.
2. **Higher-order thinking tasks:** Aim for tasks that are less prone to GenAI automation. For instance, assignments that promote decision-making, interpersonal skills, and metacognition. GenAI can be used alongside these tasks to enhance the learning experience and authenticity.
3. **Student-driven learning:** Allow students to optionally have a say in their assessments. Whether through co-creation or offering choices in topics and formats, empowering students in their learning can make a difference. For those with specific learning disabilities, this inclusion is particularly vital.
4. **Formative tasks:** Incorporate GenAI in low-stakes practice tasks that foster academic integrity and learning processes while ensuring ethical use.
5. **Training and literacy:** Equip students with the knowledge to use GenAI effectively, bridging the digital divide.
6. **Accessibility:** Where possible, incorporate free versions of GenAI technologies with safe data privilege policies to ensure all students have equal opportunities.

Next, we offer three suggestions for assessment approaches which offer solutions to various challenges and ethical considerations and opportunities discussed above.

Assessment approaches

Peer learning

Peer learning offers an avenue for incorporating GenAI into authentic formative assessment opportunities. With writing tasks, for instance, while GenAI can augment content, it is the human element within peer feedback that truly refines students' critical evaluation abilities and heightens their meta-cognitive awareness. In other tasks, GenAI can assist students in curating or distilling existing content to facilitate peer teaching sessions. Yet, it is during the peer-teaching sessions, when students step into the shoes of educators, by explaining concepts and addressing questions, that students experience deeper-learning approaches, attaining a richer understanding of the content (Hughes et al., 2022). Furthermore, seminar debates may start with AI-generated arguments. However, it is the ensuing human discourse and the dynamic interplay of feedback from educators and peers that truly improves their critical evaluative skills and understanding of the topic. To ensure the efficacy of peer interactions, it is paramount to anchor them in a psychologically safe environment, mitigating any anxieties (Hughes et al., 2022).

Processfolios

An assessment method to underline the significance of the learning journey over the outcome is through 'processfolios' (Pearson, 2021). These are a collection of artefacts that are an accompaniment to a final product that sheds light on the intricate processes culminating in those results. Such an assessment prompts students to self-reflect on their successes, pitfalls, and the strategies employed to navigate challenges. This could also provide transparency regarding GenAI use if applied. GenAI tools offer many affordances for students to complete assessments flexibly and autonomously, but it is important for metacognition and the development of agency that they can articulate how they have used these tools.

The PAIR model

The PAIR model is a framework for developing generative GenAI skills through formative assessment. It comprises four steps: problem formulation (discipline and topic specific), AI tool selection, interaction (with AI tools), and reflection (on AI tool use and evaluation of the tools) (Acar, 2023a, 2023b). It is designed to be adaptable to any discipline and to focus on core transferable skills. This model has the potential to integrate several points from our aforementioned checklist. It encompasses the development of higher-order thinking skills, provides student choice in assessment, offers a formative opportunity to teach students the ethical implications of GenAI, and ensures equity of access.

Conclusion

Now is an apt moment for educators to introspect on assessment objectives and implications for student development. Authentic assessment provides students with skills relevant to future workplaces. In conclusion, though the integration of GenAI into authentic assessments poses challenges and ethical questions, careful and thoughtful implementation can lead to a richer, more inclusive, and holistic learning experience for students.

Critical appraisal

Molly Whitbread, postgraduate taught student, King's College London

As a postgraduate Mental Health Studies student, I am aware of the rising adoption of generative AI (GenAI), and the importance for universities to consider its benefits and disadvantages in assessment design. Being directly involved in conducting focus groups with students to explore their views on using GenAI in assessment, I understand students' apprehension as well as thoughts on the potential value of using GenAI for learning and assessment. The chapter outlined unique solutions to using GenAI to enhance student learning while upholding academic standards. As a current student, this guidance is particularly useful as not only will it enable students to utilise GenAI effectively but it will also enable students to develop transferable skills for the future. A standout example for me is the 'processfolio', which encourages a meaningful learning experience, fosters innovative thinking, and improves self-reflection skills that can be applied in the context of GenAI. Furthermore, many industries are increasingly embracing GenAI. Therefore, this chapter importantly advocates teaching students to use GenAI efficiently, ethically, and with integrity to prepare students for their future careers. In conclusion, the chapter offers a useful guide for bringing GenAI into the university setting to adequately support students in assessment activities. However, continuous conversations, taking into account the perspectives of postgraduate students like myself, will be crucial for its effective implementation.

References

Acar, O.A. (2023a) *Are Your Students Ready for AI? A Four-Step Framework to Prepare Learners for a ChatGPT World.* Available at: https://hbsp.harvard.edu/inspiring-minds/are-your-students-ready-for-ai (Accessed 16 September 2023).
Acar, O.A. (2023b) *PAIR (Problem, AI, Interaction, Reflection) Framework Guidance.* Available at: www.kcl.ac.uk/about/strategy/learning-and-teaching/ai-guidance/pair-framework-guidance (Accessed 28 November 2023).
Ahmad, S.F. et al. (2023) Impact of artificial intelligence on human loss in decision making, laziness and safety in education. *Humanities and Social Sciences Communications*, 10(1), pp. 1–14. Available at: https://doi.org/10.1057/s41599-023-01787-8.
Bankins, S. and Formosa, P. (2023) The ethical implications of artificial intelligence (AI) for meaningful work. *Journal Business Ethics*, 185, pp. 725–740. Available at: https://doi.org/10.1007/s10551-023-05339-7.

Biggs, J. and Tang, C. (2007) Outcomes-based teaching and learning (OBTL) what is it. Why is it, how do we make it work. *Malaysian Journal of Learning and Instruction*, 8. Available at: https://doi.org/10.32890/mjli.8.2011.7624.

Boud, D. (2000) Sustainable assessment: Rethinking assessment for the learning society. *Studies in Continuing Education*, 22(2), pp. 151–167. Available at: https://doi.org/10.1080/713695728.

Boud, D. and Soler, R. (2016) Sustainable assessment revisited. *Assessment & Evaluation in Higher Education*, 41(3), pp. 400–413. Available at: https://doi.org/10.1080/02602938.2015.1018133.

Božić, V. (2023) Artificial intelligence as the reason and the solution of digital divide. *Language Education and Technology*, 3(2). Available at: https://langedutech.com/letjournal/index.php/let/article/view/53.

Chan, C.K.Y. (2023) *Is AI Changing the Rules of Academic Misconduct? An In-depth Look at Students' Perceptions of AI-giarism*. Available at: https://arxiv.org/ftp/arxiv/papers/2306/2306.03358.pdf (Accessed 16 September 2023).

Chan, C.K.Y. and Hu, W. (2023) *Students' Voices on Generative AI: Perceptions, Benefits, and Challenges in Higher Education*. Available at: https://doi.org/10.1186/s41239-023-00411-8 (Accessed 16 September 2023).

Chui, M., Hazan, E., Roberts, R., Singla, A., Smaje, K., Sukharevsky, A., Yee, L. and Zemmel, R. (2023) *The Economic Potential of Generative AI: The Next Productivity Frontier*. Available at: www.mckinsey.com/capabilities/mckinsey-digital/our-insights/the-economic-potential-of-generative-AI-the-next-productivity-frontier#introduction (Accessed 16 September 2023).

Dickinson, J. (2022) *What Should Higher Education Learn from the Natasha Abrahart Case?* Available at: https://wonkhe.com/blogs/what-should-higher-education-learn-from-the-natasha-abrahart-case/ (Accessed 16 September 2023).

Dobson, S. (2023) *Why Universities Should Return to Oral Exams in the AI and ChatGPT Era*. Available at: https://theconversation.com/why-universities-should-return-to-oral-exams-in-the-ai-and-chatgpt-era-203429 (Accessed 16 September 2023).

Ferrara, E. (2023) *Should ChatGPT be Biased? Challenges and Risks of Bias in Large Language Models*. Available at: https://arxiv.org/pdf/2304.03738.pdf (Accessed 16 September 2023).

Hughes, G., Upsher, R., Nobili, A., Kirkman, A., Wilson, C., Bowers-Brown, T., Foster, J., Bradley, S. and Byrom, N. (2022) *Education for Mental Health Toolkit*. Available at: www.advance-he.ac.uk/teaching-and-learning/curricula-development/education-mental-health-toolkit (Accessed 16 September 2023).

Janesick, V.J. (2006) *Authentic Assessment*. New York: Peter Lang Publishing.

Khalil, M. and Er, E. (2023) *Will ChatGPT Get You Caught? Rethinking of Plagiarism Detection*. Available at: https://doi.org/10.35542/osf.io/fnh48 (Accessed 16 September 2023).

Langreo, L. (2023) *What Skills Should Students Learn in an AI-Powered World?* Available at: www.edweek.org/technology/what-skills-should-students-learn-in-an-ai-powered-world/2023/04 (Accessed 16 September 2023).

Lim, W.M. et al. (2023) Generative AI and the future of education: Ragnarök or reformation? A paradoxical perspective from management educators.

The International Journal of Management Education, 21(2), p. 100790. Available at: https://doi.org/10.1016/j.ijme.2023.100790.

Macfarlane, B., Zhang, J. and Pun, A. (2014) Academic integrity: A review of the literature. *Studies in Higher Education*, 39(2), pp. 339–358. Available at: https://doi.org/10.1080/03075079.2012.709495.

McArthur, J. (2016) Assessment for social justice: The role of assessment in achieving social justice. *Assessment & Evaluation in Higher Education*, 41(7), pp. 967–981. Available at: https://doi.org/10.1080/02602938.2015.1053429.

McArthur, J. (2023) Rethinking authentic assessment: Work, well-being, and society. *Higher Education*, 85(1), pp. 85–101. Available at: https://doi.org/10.1007/s10734-022-00822-y.

Nkonde, M. (2023) *ChatGPT: New AI System, Old Bias?* Available at: https://mashable.com/article/chatgpt-ai-racism-bias#:~:text=With%20the%20rapid%20adoption%20of,the%20opinions%20of%20the%20writers (Accessed 16 September 2023).

Pearson, J. (2021) Assessment of agency or assessment for agency? A critical realist action research study into the impact of a processfolio assessment within UK HE preparatory courses for international students. *Educational Action Research*, 29(2), pp. 259–275. Available at: https://doi.org/10.1080/09650792.2020.1829496.

Perkins, M., Roe, J., Postma, D., McGaughran, J. and Hickerson, D. (2023) *Game of Tones: Faculty Detection of GPT-4 Generated Content in University Assessments*. Available at: https://arxiv.org/ftp/arxiv/papers/2305/2305.18081.pdf (Accessed 16 September 2023).

Russell Group (2023) *Russell Group Principles on the Use of Generative AI Tools in Education*. Available at: https://russellgroup.ac.uk/media/6137/rg_ai_principles-final.pdf (Accessed 16 September 2023).

Sambell, K., McDowell, L. and Montgomery, C. (2012) *Assessment for Learning in Higher Education*, 1st ed. New York: Routledge.

Tai, J. Mahoney, P. Ajjawi, R., Bearman, M. Dargusch, J., Dracup, M. and Harris, L. (2023) How are examinations inclusive for students with disabilities in higher education? *A Sociomaterial Analysis, Assessment & Evaluation in Higher Education*, 48(3), pp. 390–402. Available at: https://doi.org/10.1080/02602938.2022.2077910.

Waterfield, J. and West, B. (2008) Towards inclusive assessments in higher education: Case study. *Learning and Teaching in Higher Education*, 3, pp. 97–102. Available at: http://eprints.glos.ac.uk/id/eprint/3858.

13 Process not product in the written assessment

David Smith and Nigel Francis

Introduction

Writing is a central competency, indispensable given its pivotal role in academia, promoting knowledge, enhancing learning, and establishing professional credibility (Hyland, 2013). Written assignments give instructors insight into students' depth of understanding, analytical capabilities, and research skills, often being a primary means for assessing research skills, critical thinking, and understanding (Hodges, 2017). It also facilitates cognitive development and enhances communication skills, providing a lasting record of scholarly ideas. Moreover, it is a reflection tool, essential for professional advancement.

The emergence of GenAI and large language models (LLMs) provides both opportunities and challenges to written assessments. LLMs are trained on huge collections of text data sources, to capture as much human language as possible (Rudolph et al., 2023). When prompted (questioned), LLMs predict which words to respond with based on the training set. During exchanges, the GenAI recalls prior interactions to inform its next prediction, making for conversational interactions. Proponents of GenAI argue that it can improve efficiency, productivity, and information access; however, critics worry that GenAI could lead to declining academic standards (Sallam, 2023). Due to the training sets used in creating LLMs, there is an inherent bias due to prejudices in the source material that reflect historical or social inequities. With GenAI's growing integration into the writing process, written outputs will be a hybrid of human and GenAI interactions (Chen et al., 2022). Such integration, however, can also lead to inequality as many GenAI tools operate via a subscription model, which not every student can afford. Such hybrid writing also raises the question of where the boundaries of individuals' competencies and understanding are and how we develop the skills students will need for future effectiveness.

DOI: 10.4324/9781003482918-17

Essay mills and GenAI

Maintaining academic integrity is vital to ensure true authenticity in assessments (Eaton, 2021). Any misconduct, including plagiarism, collusion, or misrepresentation of sources, can severely compromise this integrity, significantly reducing the value of education. Institutions implement strict regulatory measures to combat these practices, emphasising honest learning and genuine effort. In this context, inappropriate use of GenAI tools to generate reports, essays, or other content based on prompts falls under the same regulatory framework (King and ChatGPT, 2023). GenAI tools can be helpful for brainstorming, drafting, and proofing, but over-reliance or misuse hinders skill development, limits subject-specific understanding, and contributes negatively to biases.

Process-oriented assessment (process over product)

Consider how many undergraduate written assessments you created and still reference versus how often you use the critical assessment skills you gained writing those assessments. It was the act of creation that was important (Earl, 2012). Regarding integrating GenAI into written assessments, the focus shifts to the creation process rather than the product (Rudolph et al., 2023). Assessing process over product offers many advantages, as tool usage becomes part of the output (Romova and Andrew, 2011). There are also benefits to tackling academic integrity by having assessments that build towards the final article (Sotiriadou et al., 2020). Process-oriented assessment design focuses on the learning journey and the steps taken, rather than evaluating the end product (Schreiber et al., 2016; Jeltova et al., 2007; Rodriguez et al., 2020). This approach emphasises the importance of the learning process and acknowledges how students created the final article. Assessment design can incorporate GenAI prompts, justifying tool usage, and critiquing source validity without compromising the value of learning (Brew et al., 2023). Process-oriented assessment is robust to the emergence of new technologies as it is not tied to a specific tool or platform, but records and evaluates their effective use. This is achieved through the following:

- **Continuous evaluation**: regular check-ins, feedback, and evaluations facilitated by formative submissions, seminars, and workshops.
- **Emphasis on reflection**: students reflect upon their learning processes, strategies employed, challenges encountered, and resolutions.
- **Encouraging iteration**: feedback at multiple stages allows students to revise and enhance their work, simulating real-world refinements (Schillings et al., 2023).

Assessors benefit from a holistic understanding of students' strengths, weaknesses, and learning trajectories. By incorporating iteration and feedback, students learn to handle criticism and use it constructively. Collaborative peer review also helps foster meta-cognitive and interpersonal skills. The assessment's iterative nature deters students from using essay mills, GenAIs, and LLMs and has been proven to enhance outcomes (Schreiber et al., 2016; Jeltova et al., 2007).

Process-oriented assessment design strategies

Process-oriented assessment strategies focus on student competencies and skill clusters that are needed for a particular task (Race, 2019; Littlewood, 2009). Objectives highlight behaviours that exemplify 'best practice' for a given competency (task) and inform assessment rubrics (Evans et al., 2020). In the context of academic writing, GenAI tools can support and enhance these competencies.

Research skills: demonstrated by formulating research questions, developing rigorous and effective search strategies, finding, and evaluating sources, synthesising information, and referencing.

Understanding subject matter: exemplified by gaining substantive knowledge through research and integrating ideas.

Critical thinking: characterised by analysis, evaluating evidence, constructing reasoned arguments, identifying assumptions, and drawing conclusions.

Writing skills: structuring coherent arguments, articulating ideas, using vocabulary, and style appropriately.

Assessments should be fully integrated into the taught context for students to develop these competencies and demonstrate learning outcomes. Lectures, seminars, and tutorials can aid in developing of these competencies, including ethical and appropriate use of GenAI; for instance, logging search strategies and keywords, or critically appraising content validity (Crowther et al., 2010). GenAI is incorporated into the assessment design by recording prompts and justifying how the generated text has informed the final article. Resources used are validated, and content material is critiqued whether it is human, or AI generated and biases addressed. Templated guides help structure this process, guiding students in documenting their progress towards the final product. The final written article is the by-product, and the assessment focuses on how information is collected, and future research directions. Assessments should not mandate the use of GenAI for completion, which would disadvantage students who cannot or do not want to access such tools.

Research skills – setting individualised tasks/questions

Individualised, authentic assessments provide numerous advantages compared to set titles. When students are given creative control over their work, they often feel more motivated and engaged, with a sense of ownership over the process (Shernoff et al., 2003). Allowing students to choose their own topics for assessments that align with their interests usually results in deeper involvement than assigning every student the same generic title (Parker et al., 2017).

Individualised tasks also require more original and critical thinking from students. When everyone responds to the same questions, colluding or regurgitating the same responses is more likely. However, when students must apply their knowledge to unique situations tailored to their skills and interests, individual analysis is required, bringing in higher-order skills like evaluating, synthesising, and manipulating ideas to produce an original piece.

Coming up with topics can be daunting for academics and students (Parker et al., 2017); in this setting, GenAI's brainstorming capabilities can be utilised individually, or within seminars, using well-written prompts to generate authentic topics and refine research questions.

> **You are an academic setting essay titles for first-year undergraduates studying [SUBJECT]. Give a range of potential creative topic ideas that could be used for an academic essay.**

Defining the study area through a broadly co-creational approach can be tutor-led, student-led, or collaborative, with each individual or group getting their own topic. Such individualised and authentic assessments effectively enhance student learning, reduce plagiarism, and prepare students for employment.

Research skills – finding articles

Key to writing academically is identifying and critically appraising publications (Denney and Tewksbury, 2013). The initial step involves searching for relevant information using appropriate databases. Knowing which keywords to use is the first barrier to engagement, without adequate knowledge of the subject, sourcing relevant information becomes inhibitory (Crowther et al., 2010). Seminars on search strategies and the mechanics of finding relevant literature can prepare students for the practicalities of accessing information. GenAI can help by suggesting search terms, utilising prompts that help generate keywords.

> **You are writing an academic literature review on [YOUR TOPIC]. Suggest keywords that can be used with [DATABASE] to find relevant literature.**

Students log the database(s) used, search terms, and limits, and evaluate the relevance of the results. Commentary and reflection focus on which terms gave the most relevant information against the research question.

Outside of keyword generation, several GenAI tools exist to search for research papers, aiding in consolidating ideas. Using research questions rather than keywords as the search term allows students to identify relationships between concepts and cause and effect, for example:

Does process-oriented assessment improve student outcomes?

A key competency is a rigorous and structured approach to reviewing all available evidence on a topic. Inclusion and exclusion criteria constrain conditions a study must fulfil for consideration, ensuring the review is comprehensive, replicable, and methodologically sound. Inclusion criteria verify studies' relevance to the research question, while exclusion criteria filter out irrelevant or low-quality studies that do not provide the necessary information to answer the research question. Students define their inclusion and exclusion criteria and briefly justify why papers have been included or excluded from the final output to demonstrate this process.

Understanding the subject matter

Engaging with peer-reviewed literature helps individuals acquire substantive knowledge through researching and integrating ideas. As students approach reading research papers differently from established academics (Hubbard and Dunbar, 2017), this process can become overwhelming. A core objective is ensuring students have engaged with and synthesised the material. Here, a structured approach to reading papers and extracting information can be used, with the outputs used in the final article. Students need to identify critical information against broad headings, investigate the source material, and document key aspects of the work. For example:

- What is the aim/objective?
- Describe the research/experimental design.
- Identify the outcomes measured.
- What are the main findings/conclusions?
- Critical appraisal (validity of the approach/interpretation of results).
- How will papers be used to inform your final article?

With an ever-increasing literature base, quickly identifying relevant material is time-consuming. LLMs can help synthesise information, and numerous GenAIs can either directly access research papers or accept PDF uploads.

Prompts can then be used to extract key information or common themes from multiple articles.

> **You are writing a literature review. Help me identify the main findings of the uploaded file(s).**
> **My research area is [YOUR RESEARCH QUESTION]. How does this PDF contribute to this area.**

Logging the prompts and their usage is integral to the process, reflecting the current use of GenAI in research. General knowledge gained from GenAI can also be appraised in a similar manner (Mhlanga, 2023). Here, it is key to recall how LLMs operate, because they generate text based on the most statistically likely response, and results are often predictable. Additionally, as GenAIs generate answers algorithmically, they need to comprehend the topic to avoid mistakes in their choice of words, which can lead to inaccuracies. LLMs predictions are more reliable for fundamental knowledge or core concepts due to a larger representative pool of training data for well-represented topics. Here, the outputs can be critically appraised in a similar manner, especially since they may draw from experiential and non-research evidence materials such as blogs, news articles, podcasts, and YouTube videos. This process can again be logged and recorded.

- Which GenAI was used?
- Provide original output(s).
- Comment on the quality, depth, and rigour of the output(s):

  - Consider information – (how was the output fact-checked?)
  - Potential bias – (is there an alternative viewpoint?)
  - Identify omission(s) – (is all the information present?)

- How have you/will you use the output to help write your assessment?

Effective engagement with peer-reviewed literature, facilitated by a systematic approach, is pivotal for comprehensive knowledge, forming the basis for the final piece.

Generating a product

The final written article presents reasoned arguments and conclusions, showcasing writing skills and articulation of ideas. Here, as in other areas, GenAI can scaffold the final product, enhancing the quality of the output (Nazari et al., 2021). LLMs can assist in writing an essay by providing suggestions for structure, content, and language. It turns the dreaded blank page into a workable framework to edit and expand. However, it will not write detailed articles for you (Hill-Yardin et al., 2023).

In this context, GenAI will

• provide a suggested outline, including an introduction, body paragraphs, and conclusion,
• help develop statements and the main ideas for each body paragraph,
• give suggestions for supporting evidence and examples to include,
• make suggestions for grammar, punctuation, and clarity.

Many LLMs allow direct file uploads, such as PDFs, alternatively, students can input a body of text and prompt the GenAI to process it, typically using a command like 'READ'. This command signifies to the GenAI that the text should be absorbed and used to guide subsequent responses. For instance,

I will provide a body of text for you to process. Please read this text and confirm you've done so by responding with the word READ.

Once the text is introduced, further prompts can guide the GenAI's use of that information. If students input the main body of an essay, they could use follow-up prompts to instruct the GenAI, such as

Provide a short summary of the information as an abstract.
Edit the text for clarity and remove redundancy. Give a list of changes made.

In these cases, it will be good practice to ask the students to keep drafts of their work and to counsel against overuse and reliance on GenAI tools.

Assessing the process

The assessment rubric in Table 13.1 evaluates students' competencies on multiple dimensions of their writing skills. These include the ability to navigate and search academic databases effectively, emphasising advanced search techniques. Proficiency in logging relevant keywords, requiring clear definitions and sources is assessed. Critical evaluation of the information gathered, using a template to structure students' insights, makes up a significant portion of the evaluation. The credibility of their chosen sources is scrutinised, ensuring they demonstrate discernment in their selections. Clarity and logical organisation of the work play a final pivotal role in the assessment. Lastly, the rubrics consider the overall effort and commitment students displayed throughout the task, ensuring a holistic evaluation of their performance.

Table 13.1 Assessment rubric

Criteria	Excellent	Good	Satisfactory	Needs improvement	Inadequate
Database search skills	Exhibits exceptional ability to navigate and search databases. Uses advanced search techniques effectively.	Exhibits good ability to navigate and search databases. Uses some advanced search techniques.	Exhibits basic ability to navigate and search databases. May struggle with advanced search techniques.	Has difficulty navigating and searching databases. Rarely uses advanced search techniques.	Unable to effectively navigate or search databases.
Keyword logging	Logs all relevant keywords with clear definitions and sources. Evidences understanding of the importance of each keyword.	Logs most relevant keywords with definitions and sources. Evidences understanding of most keywords.	Logs some relevant keywords. Some definitions or sources may be missing.	Logs few relevant keywords. Many definitions or sources are missing.	Does not log keywords or logs irrelevant keywords.
Critical evaluation	Critically evaluates information with depth and insight. Uses the template effectively to draw meaningful conclusions.	Critically evaluates most information. Uses the template well but may miss some nuances.	Evaluates information at a basic level. Uses the template but may not fully grasp its significance.	Struggles to critically evaluate information. Has difficulty using the template effectively.	Does not critically evaluate information or does not use the template at all.
Source credibility	Consistently selects and cites high-quality, credible sources. Displays discernment in source selection.	Selects and cites mostly credible sources. Displays good discernment in source selection.	Selects and cites some credible sources but may include some of questionable credibility.	Often selects and cites sources of questionable credibility.	Does not consider source credibility or cites entirely unreliable sources.

(*Continued*)

Criteria	Excellent	Good	Satisfactory	Needs improvement	Inadequate
Organisation and presentation	Information is organised logically and presented clearly. The template is used effectively to structure the evaluation.	Information is mostly organised and clear. The template is used well, with minor inconsistencies.	Information is somewhat organised but may lack clarity in places. The template is used inconsistently.	Information is disorganised and lacks clarity. The template is not used effectively.	Information is completely disorganised and unclear. The template is not used at all.
Overall effort	Goes above and beyond in research and evaluation. Shows exceptional effort and commitment.	Shows good effort and commitment in research and evaluation.	Shows satisfactory effort in research and evaluation.	Shows minimal effort in research and evaluation.	Does not show effort or commitment to the task.

Summary

This chapter highlights the importance of process-oriented assessment design built on authentic learning principles and the maintenance of academic integrity in the GenAI era. While LLMs can provide scaffolding during writing, overreliance risks undermining critical skills development. The proposed approach emphasises competencies like effective research, critical evaluation, and clear writing over the final product and can operate independently of GenAI use. It advocates individualised tasks, continuous feedback, and structured templates to support students in creating original work. Assessing the process rather than just the output makes AI assistance more legitimately transparent. Ultimately, education is about the skills gained along the way, of which GenAI use forms one part. By focusing on competency growth through iterative practice, we can harness GenAI's potential to augment learning while upholding the values of authentic effort and achievement.

Critical appraisal

Arya Rajan, current student (MSc Pharmacology and Biotechnology)

How were/are you involved in the practices outlined in the chapter/case study?

Throughout my academic programme, I was consistently involved in process-oriented writing tasks, requiring me to conduct thorough research, critically analyse data, and provide insightful analysis. Resultantly, I gained a wealth of knowledge and experience in academic writing, which has proven invaluable in my academic and professional pursuits.

Despite the fact that AI-driven tools such as grammar, spell, and plagiarism checkers enhanced my writing process, I made sure that my work was reflective of my abilities and contributed to a fresh perspective. As a developing academic, I found it interesting to use GenAI algorithms to generate creative ideas without compromising academic quality or integrity. Assessments focusing on the process, as described in this chapter, have been immensely helpful in promoting self-reflection and in enabling me to observe the progress and improvement in my skills over time. The literature review was an excellent reflection of process-oriented academic writing, which emphasised individual thinking and proposal development. The process facilitated confidence in my writing abilities and helped me recognise my strengths and weaknesses.

References

Brew, M., Taylor, S., Lam, R., Havemann, L. and Nerantzi, C. (2023) Towards developing AI literacy: Three student provocations on AI in higher education. *Asian Journal of Distance Education*, 18(2), pp. 1–11.

Chen, X., Zou, D., Xie, H., Cheng, G. and Liu, C. (2022) Two decades of artificial intelligence in education. *Educational Technology & Society*, 25(1), pp. 28–47.

Crowther, M., Lim, W. and Crowther, M.A. (2010) Systematic review and meta-analysis methodology. *Blood, The Journal of the American Society of Hematology*, 116(17), pp. 3140–3146.

Denney, A.S. and Tewksbury, R. (2013) How to write a literature review. *Journal of Criminal Justice Education*, 24(2), pp. 218–234.

Earl, L.M. (2012) *Assessment as Learning: Using Classroom Assessment to Maximize Student Learning*. Thousand Oaks: Corwin Press.

Eaton, S.E. (2021) *Plagiarism in Higher Education: Tackling Tough Topics in Academic Integrity*. Santa Barbara: ABC-CLIO.

Evans, D.L., Bailey, S.G., Thumser, A.E., Trinder, S.L., Winstone, N.E. and Bailey, I.G. (2020) The biochemical literacy framework: Inviting pedagogical innovation in higher education. *FEBS Open Bio*, 10(9), pp. 1720–1736.

Hill-Yardin, E.L., Hutchinson, M.R., Laycock, R. and Spencer, S.J. (2023) A Chat (GPT) about the future of scientific publishing. *Brain, Behavior, and Immunity*, 110, pp. 152–154.

Hodges, T.S. (2017) Theoretically speaking: An examination of four theories and how they support writing in the classroom. *The Clearing House: A Journal of Educational Strategies, Issues and Ideas*, 90(4), pp. 139–146.

Hubbard, K.E. and Dunbar, S.D. (2017) Perceptions of scientific research literature and strategies for reading papers depend on academic career stage. *PLoS One*, 12(12), p. e0189753.

Hyland, K. (2013) Writing in the university: Education, knowledge and reputation. *Language Teaching*, 46(1), pp. 53–70.

Jeltova, I., Birney, D., Fredine, N., Jarvin, L., Sternberg, R.J. and Grigorenko, E.L. (2007) Dynamic assessment as a process-oriented assessment in educational settings. *Advances in Speech-Language Pathology*, 9(4), pp. 273–285.

King, M.R. and ChatGPT (2023) A conversation on artificial intelligence, chatbots, and plagiarism in higher education. *Cellular and Molecular Bioengineering*, 16(1), pp. 1–2.

Littlewood, W. (2009) Process-oriented pedagogy: Facilitation, empowerment, or control? *ELT Journal*, 63(3), pp. 246–254.

Mhlanga, D. (2023) *Open AI in Education, the Responsible and Ethical Use of ChatGPT Towards Lifelong Learning. Education, the Responsible and Ethical Use of ChatGPT Towards Lifelong Learning*, 11 February. SSRN. Available at: https://doi.org/10.2139/ssrn.4354422.

Nazari, N., Shabbir, M.S. and Setiawan, R. (2021) Application of artificial intelligence powered digital writing assistant in higher education: Randomized controlled trial. *Heliyon*, 7(5).

Parker, F., Novak, J. and Bartell, T. (2017) To engage students, give them meaningful choices in the classroom. *Phi Delta Kappan*, 99(2), pp. 37–41.

Race, P. (2019) *The Lecturer's Toolkit: A Practical Guide to Assessment, Learning and Teaching*. Abingdon: Routledge.

Rodriguez, J.G., Hunter, K.H., Scharlott, L.J. and Becker, N.M. (2020) A review of research on process-oriented guided inquiry learning:

Implications for research and practice. *Journal of Chemical Education*, 97(10), pp. 3506–3520.

Romova, Z. and Andrew, M. (2011) Teaching and assessing academic writing via the portfolio: Benefits for learners of English as an additional language. *Assessing Writing*, 16(2), pp. 111–122.

Rudolph, J., Tan, S. and Tan, S. (2023) ChatGPT: Bullshit spewer or the end of traditional assessments in higher education? *Journal of Applied Learning and Teaching*, 6(1).

Sallam, M. (2023) *ChatGPT Utility in Healthcare Education, Research, and Practice: Systematic Review on the Promising Perspectives and Valid Concerns, Healthcare 2023*. Basel: MDPI, p. 887.

Schillings, M., Roebertsen, H., Savelberg, H. and Dolmans, D. (2023) A review of educational dialogue strategies to improve academic writing skills. *Active Learning in Higher Education*, 24(2), pp. 95–108.

Schreiber, N., Theyssen, H. and Schecker, H. (2016) Process-oriented and product-oriented assessment of experimental skills in physics: A comparison. In *Insights from Research in Science Teaching and Learning: Selected Papers from the ESERA 2013 Conference 2016*, Springer, pp. 29–43.

Shernoff, D.J., Csikszentmihalyi, M., Shneider, B. and Shernoff, E.S. (2003) Student engagement in high school classrooms from the perspective of flow theory. *School Psychology Quarterly*, 18(2), p. 158.

Sotiriadou, P., Logan, D., Daly, A. and Guest, R. (2020) The role of authentic assessment to preserve academic integrity and promote skill development and employability. *Studies in Higher Education*, 45(11), pp. 2132–2148.

14 Sustainable and ethical GenAI for the common good

Looking back and forward

Sue Beckingham, Jenny Lawrence, Stephen Powell, and Peter Hartley

Introduction

Bernard Marr describes GenAI as

> one of the most powerful, transformative technologies that humans have ever had access to. It's right up there with the emergence of the internet. Seriously.
>
> (Marr, 2024a)

This quote comes from the most recent book we have found at the time of writing (early 2024) that reviews the impact of GenAI and AI more generally on a wide range of sectors. While we believe that some of the claims about 'AI's transformational impact' may be exaggerated, many respected experts share similar endorsements of GenAI's potential. For example, on his personal blog, Bill Gates (co-founder of Microsoft) described the development of AI as

> fundamental as the creation of the microprocessor, the personal computer, the Internet, and the mobile phone. It will change the way people work, learn . . . and communicate with each other.
>
> (Gates, 2023)

Gates wrote this after seeing an earlier version of GPT demonstrated by the OpenAI company. This technology moved from niche applications to mass availability and widespread public acceptance in well under a year, after OpenAI released their free access version – ChatGPT – in November 2022. Anyone with an adequate internet connection could use text-based GenAI, albeit with some restrictions or limitations depending on where they were and the level of demand for the application.

Both Microsoft and Google responded by announcing their commitment to embed AI in *all* their major products. This opened the floodgates – a deluge of

DOI: 10.4324/9781003482918-18

new and established apps using GenAI, both open source and proprietary, and from both well-established companies and new start-ups.

In early 2024, we find GenAI features in our main everyday software applications, provided we have access to (and can afford) the necessary licence. With new GenAI software, we can use text prompts to generate outputs in various formats, including images (2D and 3D), music, and video; and we can translate from image, audio, and video to text. New hardware offers new opportunities, including advances in virtual and augmented reality, and new portable devices.

What can we learn from AI's history so far?

A few key milestones and trends provide clues to likely futures.

Serious attempts to simulate human intelligence date from the mid-1950s. The following decades saw cycles of 'enthusiasm' and 'disinterest' punctuated by notable signs of progress such as the software that defeated world-class players of Chess and Go (Mitchell, 2020). The use of 'traditional AI' in this context was able to learn and predict moves based on *pattern recognition*. GenAI excels at *pattern creation* and can provide new ways of playing chess (Marr, 2024a).

Current levels of investment, coupled with significant advances in GenAI technology, mean that this erratic 'stop-go' development will *not* be repeated. GenAI will become more powerful and efficient, especially when it can search for recent/current or real-time events.

Chatbots – software which engages you in 'conversation' – also have significant history, dating from the 1960s when 'Eliza' simulated conversations with a psychotherapist (Weizenbaum, 1976; Rossen, 2023). Improvements in speech recognition software mean chatbots can respond vocally, as in everyday apps like Alexa and Siri, and auto-completion in texts and emails. These are destined to become much more powerful thanks to GenAI.

A common economic pattern emerged during 2023, also with profound consequences – the availability of GenAI software in two or more versions. Typically, we see a free or trial version with major functions and possibly limited access, and a paid version for subscribers – with more powerful features. The quest for sustainable business models for this technology has obvious implications for student (and staff) access and availability. There are also implications for data security. 'Free' applications may be primarily interested in gathering your data – the low or no cost is the incentive to get us involved.

The notion that we can all have a 'personal virtual assistant' powered by GenAI is now technically feasible. It has been enthusiastically promoted by organisations as diverse as Microsoft (Warren, 2023) and the Khan Academy (Khan Labs, 2024). But, for educators seeking to harness these developments for learning and teaching, some very serious questions remain unanswered, including the following:

- Can all our educational institutions afford to support this sort of provision given current economic limitations?
- Can we offer such a facility to all our students, overcoming obstacles of access and accessibility?
- Can we be assured that data security, privacy concerns, and potential biases in GenAI algorithms will be addressed?
- What might the impact of virtual assistants be on human social interaction?
- What is our ethical stance on the environmental costs of running GenAI?

Future applications and implications for higher education

Previous chapters have identified significant major themes which will be on the agenda for all HEIs over the next decade. To achieve the necessary whole-institution approach, collaboration is needed from educational developers, information technologists, data security specialists, access and participation experts, and quality assurance colleagues.

Issues include how to ensure that

1. institutions remain agile and responsive to increasingly fast-paced technological developments and regulatory changes,
2. institutions incorporate flexible quality processes and speedy data-security checks for new applications as they emerge and are updated
3. all students and staff have equitable access to the technology which is necessary for their professional and personal development,
4. students and staff involved in teaching and supporting learning all develop and sustain appropriate levels of GenAI literacy,
5. GenAI is used effectively within teaching, learning, and assessment in different subject disciplines, taking a whole-programme approach to ensure consistency across the students' programme.

To respond to these agendas, we suggest that all institutions need to develop coherent and effective approaches in (at least) the following areas:

Frameworks for GenAI application

Institutionally focused frameworks can provide clear and consistent guidance for teaching staff and students about the ethically acceptable use of GenAI which can be applied in specific subject areas and courses/programmes (e.g. Hillier, 2023).

To provide an inclusive experience for all students, approaches such as the Universal Design for Learning framework (CAST, 2024) provide guidance on how to best present information to make it accessible for all (Farrelly and Baker, 2023).

Teaching methods and approaches

Staff and students need to adopt effective and ethical methods and approaches in their study and learning.

For example, a number of university tutors now use the PAIR approach where students incorporate GenAI in four steps, as explained in Chapter 12 (also see Acar, 2023 and Cooner's (2023, 2024) use of PAIR with social work students and his more general thoughts on ChatGPT on his YouTube channel).

Sharples (2023, p. 162) proposes various roles for text-based GenAI in cooperative and social learning, such as possibility engine, Socratic opponent, collaboration coach, co-designer, exploratorium, and storyteller. Considering these roles can prove valuable in addressing the problem or task.

Assessment design and strategies

GenAI has triggered a wave of critical reassessment among teaching staff, with a recent small survey of American tutors revealing that virtually all the staff had adjusted their assessment practices, although some reverted to previous approaches rather than searching out more student-centred, developmental models. In Chapters 11 and 13, the authors explain how GenAI can be integrated within existing frameworks and best practices to create authentic, relevant assessments that benefit both students and educators.

Better understanding of student use and perspectives

To make the most effective use of GenAI, a more sophisticated understanding of student attitudes, expectations, and existing or developing practices is needed. We have seen in previous chapters that these can vary considerably, and we can also see them changing and becoming more sophisticated.

We all need to be aware of developments here, as in the 'ChatGPT and Me' project led by Drumm et al. (2023), gathering anonymised student attitudes to GenAI and their own learning and assessment while they are studying.

Access to technology and availability

Currently, some staff might rely on students using free versions of GenAI platforms. However, relying on free software is not a sustainable or ethical long-term strategy for either staff or students. Institutions need to establish baseline provisions for both groups to ensure some equality of access. While parallels exist with other computer costs for students, addressing the inequality in access to essential GenAI-powered software should be a priority.

The costs of GenAI in HE

While the consideration of financial costs is not a prime focus of this book, we cannot avoid this 'elephant in the room'. When we sent this text to Routledge in January 2024, the long-term situation regarding the costs of adoption of GenAI in HEIs was unclear.

Our conversations with several UK HEIs have confirmed that the potential long-term costs of GenAI pose a significant issue. In an ideal world, we will see inter-institutional collaboration to explore GenAI's effectiveness in different contexts. But this may be difficult given the competitive structures which we see, at least in UK HEIs.

And, we may be witnessing the dawn of a new era of competitive struggles between universities to offer the 'best deal' for students in terms of their access to GenAI. Also, in January 2024, the OpenAI company announced their ground-breaking university-wide agreement with Arizona State University (ASU). In their announcement on ASU News, the University suggested that this was

> setting a new precedent for how universities enhance learning, creativity and student outcomes.
>
> (Davis, 2024)

We will see how this develops over 2024/25 and beyond.

Staff development and support

Many readers will be focused on how to equip educators to meet challenges and adopt/adapt pedagogic practices elaborated in this book. During our careers in teaching and educational development, we have wrestled with this challenge in different institutions. We suggest three crucial principles that, we believe, can unlock staff development success:

- Offer different channels of engagement for staff at all levels, including educational leaders and those who teach and support learning, professional services, librarians, and technical staff.
  Relevant channels include web resources, independent study, workshops, showcases and in-depth discussion, and collaborative projects to get staff involved and to cater for different levels of commitment and enthusiasm.

- Align guidance and interpretations closely to institutional policy and national regulations, emphasising the importance of informed academic judgement based on evidence-based practice.
- Empower staff and course teams to own their curriculum, teaching, and assessment practices so they can adapt them to meet the needs of their students and their discipline.

Because GenAI affects every subject area across HE, this does give us opportunities for significant cross-institutional and inter-departmental collaboration, but only if we grasp the opportunity and allocate the time and resource to do this justice. As argued by Selwyn (2024, p. 12), educators need to be part of the conversations to consider

> new forms of AI that emphasise human elements of learning and teaching, that are sympathetic to education contexts, that involve educators in their conception, development and implementation, and are based around values of trust, care and align with shared educations vision.

Where do we go from here?

As our final contribution to this debate, we offer an updated concept map we have used across the sector (Figure 14.1, adapted from Beckingham and Hartley, 2023).

You can read the map by following the arrows from the top left which take you to five components for an effective institutional strategy for GenAI.

As well as taking the obvious steps to provide sensible regulations and coherent staff and technical development, institutions must consider how they engage staff and students in future developments. We suggest that every institution needs a coherent structure which enables staff and students to work together on experiments and investigations with new GenAI in order to pilot and trial different approaches – what we have called the 'collaborative sandpit'.

Institutions with already-developed initiatives in 'students as change agents' (JISC, n.d.) and/or co-creation opportunities (Bovill, 2019, 2020) have a good starting point. However, all institutions have an opportunity with GenAI to introduce profound changes in the ways we work with students which will fully engage them in our joint futures.

And finally: How will the technology develop in the next decade? And what does this mean for HE?

These questions crop up in every GenAI workshop/event.

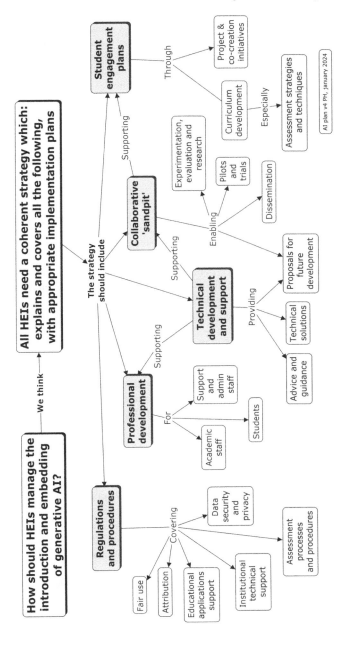

Figure 14.1 Concept map recommending how Higher Education Institutions (HEIs) can respond effectively to GenAI.

The pace of technological development makes it difficult if not impossible to offer definitive answers; therefore, we suggest a few specific questions about GenAI with practical implications for HE over the next few years.

If you are a tutor or educational developer in HE, then you are invited to use these questions with students and colleagues to assess developments and progress. These questions (and others) could be a useful starting point for a 'sandpit' discussion and/or workshop.

How will GenAI affect future jobs and employment?

While this question has obvious implications for our students' futures, it also raises important questions about the relevance of the curriculum we offer them now.

Unfortunately, there is no easy answer. Estimates on future impact vary widely.

Consider the following paragraph from Bernard Marr's review of the World Economic Forum Annual Meeting in Davos in January 2024:

> The International Monetary Fund's "Gen-AI: Artificial Intelligence and the Future of Work" report, unveiled at Davos, paints a stark picture: up to 60% of jobs in advanced economies are at risk due to AI.
>
> (Marr, 2024b)

While this meeting was debating that report, we noted the BBC interview where the Governor of the Bank of England is quoted as saying:

> 'Artificial intelligence will not be the "mass destroyer" of jobs, . . .'
>   'economies adapt, jobs adapt, and we learn to work with it',
>   adding that 'I think you get a better result by people with machines than with machines on their own'.
>
> (Faragher, 2024)

So, the jury is out.

A number of studies and analyses now suggest that the *combination* of human and machine 'intelligence' is a more effective (and safer) strategy than relying on either one alone (Daugherty and Wilson, 2018).

Deciding on the best balance between human effort and GenAI capability is possibly the most important challenge for education at all levels. And a very timely and relevant project/research opportunity for our students.

What will be the next generation of GenAI tools?

We suggest the following trends will continue:

Improvements in GenAI image software

GenAI produced significant improvements in image quality through 2023 and 2024. This will continue, while issues with previous software are resolved – for example, accurate representation of people's hands and faces, and correct spelling of text within images.

New interfaces for GenAI interactions

Obvious examples include 'talking to GenAI' on your smartphone and using new generations of translation apps to prepare messages and have conversations in multiple languages.

Further developments of GPTs

For example, ChatGPT Plus subscribers now have access to the 'GPT Store' where users offer specialist GPTs they have built themselves, without needing coding expertise.

Subscribers can also now use GPTs in a sequence to create multiple outputs – for example, a text response, an image, a PowerPoint slide, and a video – all from the same initial text prompt.

Developments in internet search

Users of tools like ChatGPT, Bing/Copilot, or Gemini are now accustomed to receiving full-text answers to searches and are increasingly presented with further resources and suggestions. Some commentators suggest that this signals the 'end of Google Search' (Wu et al., 2024).

How far will GenAI be adopted by tutors in universities?

We know more courses and tutors will use GenAI. We anticipate this will reflect a growing sophistication about its role to support and enhance student learning. For example, Dan Sarofian-Butin (2024) uses the analogy of ChatGPT as a 'learning satnav' for students, using it as his 'formal teaching assistant'. He describes his use of ChatGPT as an essential tool to help students acquire the 'road map' they need to become proficient writers.

How will students use GenAI in future?

The year 2024 will probably be remembered as the year when student use of GenAI reached its 'tipping point' – the point when it moved to general use and acceptance.

We believe we have now reached that point, as evidenced by the most recent study of student practice we could find – the UK-wide survey by HEPI and Kortext (Freeman, 2024). This survey found that 'More than half of students (53%) have used generative AI to help them prepare assessments'. Students were very aware of ethical concerns but there were some worrying findings:

> More than a third of students who have used generative AI (35%) do not know how often it produces made-up facts, statistics, or citations.
>
> ('hallucinations')

> A 'digital divide' in AI use may be emerging.

If we accept that this data is reasonably representative of the wider student population *and* we recognise that the percentages of uses and users will increase over the next few years, then we must prepare for a future where

- *every* student is familiar with the benefits and limitations of GenAI,
- every student is prepared to use GenAI ethically and effectively,
- only a very small minority of students are ignoring ethical issues,
- there is a real and growing digital divide which we need to counteract,
- students receive support for and access to GenAI which is both fair and equitable.

We hope that this book has offered you some helpful suggestions and ideas for this journey.

References

Acar, O.A. (2023) *Are Your Students Ready for AI? A Four-Step Framework to Prepare Learners for a ChatGPT World*. Harvard Business School Publishing. Available at: https://hbsp.harvard.edu/inspiring-minds/are-your-students-ready-for-ai? (Accessed 3 January 2024).

Beckingham, S. and Hartley, P. (2023) Reshaping higher education learning, teaching and assessment through artificial intelligence: What do we need to know, do, and be concerned about? In *Pedagogic Research Conference*, University of Liverpool.

Bovill, C. (2019) A co-creation of learning and teaching typology: What kind of co-creation are you planning or doing? *International Journal for Students as Partners*, 3(2), pp. 91–98. Available at: https://doi.org/10.15173/ijsap.v3i2.3953.

Bovill, C. (2020) *Co-Creating Learning and Teaching: Towards relational pedagogy in Higher Education*. St Albans: Critical Publishing.

CAST (2024) *About Universal Design for Learning*. Available at: www.cast.org/impact/universal-design-for-learning-udl (Accessed 30 January 2024).

Cooner, T.S. (2023) *ChatGPT: How It can Boost Your Academic Studies.* Available at: https://youtu.be/I1OJEcXXj7s (Accessed 14 November 2023).

Cooner, T.S. (2024) *YouTube Channel and AI in Education Videos.* Available at: www.youtube.com/@tscooner (Accessed 30 January 2024).

Daugherty, P.R. and Wilson, H.J. (2018) *Human + Machine: Reimagining Work in the Age of AI.* Cambridge, Massachusetts: Harvard Business Review Press.

Davis, A. (2024) A new collaboration with Open AI charts the future of AI in higher education. *ASU News.* Available at: https://news.asu.edu/20240118-university-news-new-collaboration-openai-charts-future-ai-higher-education (Accessed 23 January 2024).

Drumm, L., Illingworth, S., Graham, C., Calabrese, P., Taylor, S., Dencer-Brown, I. and van Knippenberg, I. (2023) *'ChatGPT & Me' Student Padlet Data with Reactions.* [Dataset]. Available at: https://doi.org/10.17869/enu.2023.3200728 (Accessed 3 February 2023).

Faragher, J. (2024) Bank of England and lords committee urge employers to adapt to AI. *Personnel Today.* Available at: www.personneltoday.com/hr/ai-impact-on-jobs-bank-of-england/ (Accessed 2 February 2023).

Farrelly, T. and Baker, N. (2023) Generative artificial intelligence: Implications and considerations for higher education practice. *Education Sciences,* 13(11), p. 1109. Available at: https://doi.org/10.3390/educsci13111109.

Freeman, J. (2024) New HEPI policy note finds more than half of students have used generative AI for help on assessments – but only 5% likely to be using AI to cheat. *HEPI.* Available at: www.hepi.ac.uk/2024/02/01/new-hepi-policy-note-finds-more-than-half-of-students-have-used-generative-ai-for-help-on-assessments-but-only-5-likely-to-be-using-ai-to-cheat/ (Accessed 1 February 2024).

Gates, B. (2023) The age of AI has begun. *GatesNotes.* Available at: www.gatesnotes.com/The-Age-of-AI-Has-Begun (Accessed 23 January 2024).

Hillier, M.A. (2023) Proposed AI literacy framework. *TECHE.* Available at: https://teche.mq.edu.au/2023/03/a-proposed-ai-literacy-framework/ (Accessed 30 January 2024).

JISC (n.d.) *What is the Change Agent's Network?* Available at: https://can.jiscinvolve.org/wp/what-is-can/ (Accessed 30 January 2024).

Khan Labs (2024) *World-Class AI for Education.* Available at: www.khanacademy.org/khan-labs (Accessed 3 February 2024).

Marr, B. (2024a) *Generative AI in Practice.* Chichester: Wiley.

Marr, B. (2024b) AI everywhere: The unmissable highlights from Davos 2024. *Forbes.* Available at: www.forbes.com/sites/bernardmarr/2024/01/22/ai-everywhere-the-unmissable-highlights-from-davos-2024/ (Accessed 31 January 2024).

Mitchell, M. (2020) *Artificial Intelligence: A Guide for Thinking Humans.* London: Pelican Books.

Rossen, J. (2023) *Please Tell Me Your Problem: Remembering ELIZA, the Pioneering 60s Chatbot.* Available at: www.mentalfloss.com/posts/eliza-chatbot-history (Accessed 3 February 2024).

Sarofian-Butin, D. (2024) As a learning satnav, ChatGPT puts students on road to success. *Times Higher Education.* Available at: www.

timeshighereducation.com/opinion/used-learning-co-pilot-chatgpt-puts-students-road-success (Accessed 1 February 2024).

Selwyn, N. (2024) On the limits of artificial intelligence (AI) in education. *Nordisk tidsskrift for pedagogikk og kritikk*, 10(1). Available at: https://doi.org/10.23865/ntpk.v10.6062.

Sharples, M. (2023) Towards social generative AI for education: Theory, practices and ethics. *Learning: Research and Practice*, 9(2), pp, 159–167. Available at: https://doi.org/10.1080/23735082.2023.2261131.

Warren, T. (2023) Microsoft announces windows copilot, an AI 'personal assistant' for Windows 11. *The Verge*. Available at: www.theverge.com/2023/5/23/23732454/microsoft-ai-windows-11-copilot-build (Accessed 3 February 2024).

Weizenbaum, J. (1976) *Computer Power and Human Reason: From Judgment to Calculation*. New York: W. H. Freeman and Company.

Wu, J., Batchelor, L., Bosa, D. and Gilbert, M. (2024) Is this the end of Google Search? How the giant could lose its lead. *CNBC Techcheck*. Available at: www.cnbc.com/video/2024/02/02/is-this-the-end-of-google-search-how-the-giant-could-lose-its-lead.html (Accessed 3 February 2024).

Index

Note: Page numbers in **bold** indicate a table on the corresponding page.

For Product Safety Concerns and Information please contact our EU
representative GPSR@taylorandfrancis.com Taylor & Francis Verlag GmbH,
Kaufingerstraße 24, 80331 München, Germany

Printed and bound by CPI Group (UK) Ltd, Croydon, CR0 4YY
08/06/2025
01897011-0005